Check List

FOR A

Perfect Wedding

CHECK LIST

FOR A

PERFECT WEDDING

Newly Revised and Expanded
Fifth Edition

Barbara Lee Follett

MAIN STREET BOOKS

DOUBLEDAY
New York   London   Toronto   Sydney   Auckland

A MAIN STREET BOOK
PUBLISHED BY DOUBLEDAY
a division of Bantam Doubleday Dell Publishing Group, Inc.
1540 Broadway, New York, New York 10036

DOUBLEDAY, MAIN STREET, and the portrayal of a building
with a tree are trademarks of Doubleday,
a division of Bantam Doubleday Dell Publishing Group, Inc.

Original Edition: 1961
Revised Editions: 1967, 1973, 1986, 1993

Book design by Tasha Hall

Library of Congress Cataloging-in-Publication Data

Follett, Barbara Lee.
Check list for a perfect wedding / Barbara Lee Follett. —
5th ed.
p.   cm.
"A Main Street book."
1. Wedding etiquette.   I. Title.
BJ2051.F6   1993
395′.22—dc20   92-16502
                                                        CIP

ISBN 0-385-46815-6

To My Family

TERI
the delightful bride

BEN
the generous father of the bride

LEE
the helpful and encouraging son
(and occasional comedy relief)

MOTHER AND FATHER
always an inspiration

Contents

"PERFECT"

★ *Complete*
★ *Flawless*
★ *Precisely appropriate*
★ *Right*
★ *Impeccable*
★ *Unblemished*
★ *Free from omission*
★ *Excellent*

Check List

for a

Perfect Wedding

First Thoughts

You are engaged! Best wishes to you and your fiancé for all the happiness in the world—now and always.

Now the exciting and sometimes hectic fun of planning the wedding is before you. This book takes over to help with every aspect.

Has your engagement already been announced? If not, refer to page 29 for a full guide to various ways to make the announcement, notify newspapers, and attend to other preliminaries. If these have been taken care of, then on with the main event—Your Wedding.

Wedding plans equal lists, and lists equal efficiency. This Check List has already compiled your lists for you. It gives you the perfect formula for your perfect wedding—correct, complete, and in chronological order. Just follow the items of instruction one by one as they are listed.

When you have taken care of each item *to fit your taste and pocketbook,* check it off, or if an item does not fit your plan, *check it off and forget it.* When you have considered and attended to all the items, you will have your perfect wedding with a minimum of confusion.

While this check list is addressed to happy brides-to-be the world over, it is designed equally for brides' mothers. Sometimes it is difficult to tell where the bride's tasks end and where her mother's begin.

My own role was that of mother-of-the-bride, and

I found that while the bride blissfully floated along on her personal cloud, many of the more earthy tasks fell to me. We have all attended many weddings, but we tend to overlook the details. That is as it *should* be. The machinery behind a carefully planned wedding is never evident, but it is always there.

How many mothers of a bride-to-be have awakened in the middle of the night startled by unanswered questions! "How do I cope with Ted's mother *and* his stepmother?" or "What number can I give the caterer when so many guests still haven't responded?" or "What is Sue supposed to do with seven salad bowls?"

Having found the answers to these and every other question that needed answering, I noted them.

I saved my check list at the request of many friends who sensed that the serenity and beauty of our daughter's wedding could have been achieved only through meticulous planning. From my notes, followed by deep personal research, came the original edition of *Check List for a Perfect Wedding*.

It is my good fortune—and yours, too, I hope—that Doubleday approved periodic revisions and updatings that have taken place over the years.

Continual research, questions from friends and strangers, and my question-and-answer columns have kept me in touch with a variety of problems and situations from diverse sources.

Now on our way toward two million copies, we celebrate with yet another newly revised, updated, and extensively expanded edition.

Brides and their mothers will know that by the wedding day it is too late to change plans, remedy mistakes, or add forgotten details. Rely on this new book with confidence, and know that *all* will be done, and done *well*.

There are those rare people who thrive under last-minute pressure. They have the physical and emotional makeup that lets them work under that kind of tension, and miraculously, some get by. If you are like that, Bravo! and I hope your luck continues. But most of us learn to expect the unexpected and that we must provide time for it.

This leeway time is essential in planning a wedding and reception, when so many separate, isolated details must meld at the zero hour—the wedding day.

How often I hear, "Can you believe it! I've called four of the best photographers, and they've been booked for months!" Another wail comes from a bride-to-be who just discovered she was too late for delivery of the gown she "adored." Six months is none too soon to order your gown, reserve the church and reception locale, and engage the services you need.

The traditional wedding in all its glory is more popular than ever. Among other things, this means you might choose to wear your mother's wedding gown (see p. 49). Make your plans, but always remember your objective—a happy, serene, memorable day, not a stage production.

Magazine and newspaper articles headline the high cost of weddings. Yes! They can be, and often are, but not necessarily. Feel confident that the elaborateness and cost of your wedding will not make it outstanding, so do not put a financial strain on your parents or yourself. With much thought combined with careful planning item by item, you can attain your flawless wedding while staying within your means.

Never economize on effort and planning. They are the essential factors that will make your wedding beautiful.

Instead of a special chapter on economizing, you

will find throughout the book numerous ideas for prudently keeping expenses down. Over and over the book suggests such workable alternatives as "engage *or* ask kind friends . . . ," "hire *or* appoint a relative or friend . . . ," "buy *or* rent *or* borrow . . ." Those choices and decisions apply to many of the components. For example, consider the flowers for the church and reception. Maybe you feel inadequate or timid about arranging them yourself, but among your friends, there must be one who is talented in that art. That person might be delighted to arrange the flowers that were picked from another friend's garden. What more personal, loving, and priceless wedding presents could they both give you!

Traditionally the bride's family pays all the wedding and reception expenses, with but a few exceptions that are considered to be the groom's responsibility (see p. 130).

We sometimes find, however, the groom's parents taking an active part in the plans and assuming half the cost (see p. 147), and we often see bridal couples who are on their own, paying for their own weddings. No matter how the finances are handled, keep your clear-cut objective in mind.

In our melting pot society, coupled with the ease and frequency of travel, marriages sometimes bring together persons of different cultures. Each has something of value to contribute—perhaps incorporating a custom or tradition from each culture. To do so is not a compromise, but rather, a meaningful addition to your ceremony, and to your lives together.

If you or your groom-to-be were previously married, you will find an entire chapter written just for *you*. It starts on page 158. If this will be your husband's second marriage but your first, plan any style wedding that pleases you both.

Weddings *should* be fun, and yours *will* be if your nerves are not frayed by too many details. Go to sleep each night with the assurance that when you awaken the next day, you have only to consult your Check List. It will do the worrying for you. Relax. Enjoy the excitement and have fun.

Barbara Lee Follett
(MRS. BENJAMIN FOLLETT)

The Right Start

Several things are essential in planning a wedding. First is this Check List. Second is a file-card system, which is absolutely indispensable. Third is a calendar. There is one in the back of this book. Fourth is a notebook in which to register gifts as they arrive.

Get plenty of three-by-five filing cards and a file box with alphabetical dividers. Now start on the guest list. Your list will start with your own family and friends. Perhaps your father or mother want to include a few business friends who are personally close to them. And their spouses, too, of course. The groom and his parents will add their lists. Make out an individual filing card for each prospective guest. Example:

Carter, Mr. and Mrs. John
810 Fifth Avenue
San Francisco
California 94406

File the cards alphabetically. Keep going over the cards, and *think* as you go. You will remember that Mr. and Mrs. Carter have a daughter who is eighteen. She should receive a separate invitation (do not economize on this), so type a card for her too. The bridesmaids may have brothers and sisters and parents to be invited individually (never put "and family" on the invitations), and their cards will go into the correct place in the file box.

Some brides have found it handy to use different colored file cards to distinguish between their own and the groom's list or those to receive announcements or invitations.

As you file the cards in alphabetical order, you might discover duplications you could otherwise overlook. The flexibility of the file system will save you from copying lists endlessly. You can mark the corners of the cards with symbols, such as C-O for "church only," C-R for "church and reception," A for "announcement only," or whatever suits your individual plan.

After using the cards to address the invitations (mark each card as you address), make an alphabetical master list, using only last names. I taped my list to the back of a door convenient to the place where I open my mail. This is your check list for noting responses. As the responses arrive, cross off the names of those who regret, and note the *number* of those who accept. For example: 2 Carter. This method will make it easy to arrive at a final total.

Duplicate the list for the groom's parents. They will appreciate the chance to familiarize themselves with the names of those they don't already know, so they will feel at ease at the reception.

Personal computers, with their many, almost magical functions, are ideal for keeping records, and categorizing everything from guest lists and services to budgeting expenses—even working out charts for timing. When you are asked for a list of friends to invite to a party in your honor, just rely on your trusty word processing program to bring forth as many printouts as you need.

Brides and their mothers, while living on opposite coasts or distant continents, have been known to successfully plan entire weddings by exchanging their computer disks for updating, revising, and adding personal comments.

And then there is the fax if you need an instant exchange of information!

Have a divider in your file box labeled "Services," for the names, addresses, and phone numbers of the florist, caterer, photographer, and others. Although you will also note the information in this book, it is advisable to keep it in both places for easy reference.

When a gift arrives, list it by number in your gift register. Tape a duplicate number to the gift. Be sure to record the name of the store in the register. This will be a help in checking errors and is indispensable if gifts have to be returned. (Exchanges are permissible provided you use discretion.) It is helpful to save the boxes of gifts you know will have to be exchanged.

When you check your file card for the address of the donor to whom you are writing a thank-you letter, record the gift on the file card and the date you mailed your thank-you note. This will give you a quick reference and will help you meet many a diplomatic crisis. A flip of the file will instantly remind you of the treasure Great-aunt Agatha sent.

Keep up with your handwritten thank-you notes—otherwise they can become a burden instead of a pleasure. If the gift is from Mr. and Mrs. Giftsender, address your thanks to them both. Include your fiancé's name in the body of the letter ("Bob and I will love to use the beautiful glasses . . ."), but sign only your own name. Use paper that is unadorned or with your own name or monogram. It is too soon to use the groom's initials.

Although you would never request money, you might be lucky enough to receive checks from relatives. The donors will be pleased if you tell them how you plan to spend the money. You might follow this thought in your own words: "We would have had to wait so long for such an elegant lamp [or whatever], but now, thanks to your generous check. . . ."

A sharp warning: some brides have the mistaken idea that their busy schedule excuses them from writing prompt thank-you notes. This myth has been the cause of many misunderstandings and consequent criticism of the bride and her family. A donor sometimes worries that the gift was never delivered, and requests the store to put a tracer on it. To find, "yes, it was delivered," embarrasses both of you. When you think of the time, effort, and money your friends spent on you, you will agree they have every right to expect a prompt, warm, personal letter in return. Enough on this subject once and for all.

If you are going on an extended honeymoon trip, or moving to another city, it is wise to list which gifts are to be stored, exchanged, or shipped. Make these notes in your gift register. If you are away from home, you will need a list of gifts as they arrive, so you can keep up with your thank-you notes. The groom's mother will also appreciate having a copy of the gift list, so she will know what her friends have sent.

Early in your planning, arrange to give or send the groom's mother a copy of this book. Brides have discovered that if everyone uses the same source of reference, it promotes understanding and cooperation, and avoids diverse opinions and dissension "within the ranks." The groom will also need a copy. Even his best man and your maid of honor would find this reference useful.

Now on with the fun and specifics that will make your wedding joyful and perfect. . . .

The Essential Preliminaries

Allow as much time as you can for these first steps. Every step you take early does not have to be taken later—in the days when parties and showers abound. From now on, simply follow this check list. As you complete an item and record the relevant data, or decide it does not apply to your plan, *check off* the item and forget it.

These numbered items are concise reminders of everything you need to consider. They also refer you to later pages where the subjects are fully covered.

1. Decide what type of wedding you will have, the degree of formality, and the approximate size.

2. Set the date and hour for the wedding. If your budget is tight, remember that an afternoon reception does not call for as expensive a menu as at other times of day (see p. 123).

3. Reserve the church* and make certain the clergyman is available. At the same time reserve the church

---

*Because there are many edifices in which to worship or be married—temples, cathedrals, synagogues, chapels, etc.—I have used one word, *church*, throughout this book to include them all. In addition, one can be married in a home, hotel, garden, club, or hall.

I have also used one word, *clergyman*, to cover the officials of all denominations, whether they be priest, rabbi, minister, pastor, or other. One can also be married by a judge, governor, chaplain, or registrar, to name a few.

Remember the all-inclusive words—*church* and *clergyman*.

for the rehearsal (see p. 40). Note the correct full name and address of the church for invitations.

4. With your fiancé, arrange a time to meet your clergyman for a personal talk. Make a calendar note. Your talk with him might be the first of several or many sessions of premarital counseling. Some churches now mandate up to a six-month preparation period. The secretary can help with details of the wedding and rehearsal.

5. After considering the size of your guest list, decide where you will hold the reception. Note: Experience shows that approximately one-quarter of those invited will be unable to attend, so you can safely invite more than you expect to attend.

You might wonder how to find a reception locale to fit your specifications. This search is especially difficult if you are from out of town. Recommendations from friends are always helpful. Bookstores and libraries stock guides for local sites. The Chamber of Commerce and business associations also have pertinent information, or can refer you to other sources. A telephone call will elicit some cold facts, such as cost and capacity, but *be sure* to visit in person to see if the accommodations appeal to you.

6. Select the bridesmaids from among your close friends. Don't choose your maid or matron of honor "from the ranks." Decide whom you want in advance, then invite her specifically for this special position. If one of the groom's sisters is of reasonable age, invite her to be a bridesmaid. This can be the first step toward a good interfamily relationship.

Many people of experience advise against including

a flower girl or ring bearer in the wedding party. Children are notorious scene stealers. If you are willing to risk scene stealing on your big day, see p. 144.

7. Remind the groom to select his ushers and best man. Perhaps he will include one of your brothers. One usher is needed for every fifty guests. There need not be the same number of bridesmaids as ushers.

8. Copy bridesmaids' and ushers' names, addresses, and telephone numbers onto your file cards; you will need them frequently. Make duplicate lists of bridesmaids and ushers for friends who will want to include them in prewedding parties.

9. If your local newspaper welcomes engagement news, send yours. Large city papers are generally not interested, but smalltown papers usually are (see p. 30).

10. Begin the card file of wedding guests. Discuss with the groom's family the number of guests you can accommodate. If they live in the same area, they are entitled to half the guests, if they so desire. If they live far removed, they probably will not need as many invitations. Ask them to send you their list. You will need it early, so *set a deadline*.

11. If the reception is to be held in your home, begin now to plan for the garden, house décor, and cleaning of the house before the reception. (Use the blank pages at the back of this book for your notes.)

12. If the reception is to be held at a hotel, restaurant, or club, make the reservation now. You can take care of the final details later.

13. Engage the caterer and make preliminary plans. Note the name and phone number in this book and on a file card under "Services." The purpose of duplicate notations is to make all information readily available to more than one person. Note date of appointment to discuss final details—at least two weeks before the wedding and preferably sooner (see p. 60).

14. Decide if you prefer to record your wedding and reception in a photograph album or on videotape. You might decide on both after you investigate them.

Record names and phone numbers in this book and under "Services" in your card file. Set a date for a final personal or telephone conference at least three weeks before the wedding. Make a calendar note (see p. 67).

15. Engage florist. Note name and telephone number in this book and in your card file under "Services." Set a date for a conference as early as possible, but no later than three weeks before the wedding. Make a calendar note (see p. 72).

16. Arrange for music at the church. Note: Some churches provide the organist and will not permit outside musicians. Ask the fee, and arrange for payment before or after the wedding. How distracting to have to write checks on the day of the wedding! Note the musicians' names (see p. 75).

17. Engage musicians for the reception. As usual, make notations in this book and in your file. Set a date for a personal or telephone conference to select the music. Make a calendar note, and arrange for making payment either before or after the reception (see p. 76).

18. Hire limousines or arrange with friends to take the wedding party to and from the church. *Important:* Be certain to arrange transportation from the church for the groom's parents so the receiving line can start promptly. Note names and telephone numbers under "Services" and in this book, as usual. Arrange for payment either before or after the wedding day (see p. 78).

19. Shop for your wedding gown and veil. Six months is none too early if your gown has to be ordered. You might be lucky and find one available in stock, or, if your budget so dictates, consider a rental gown. (For further information, see p. 49.)

20. Shop for mother-of-the-bride's dress. It is sometimes difficult to find the perfect dress to complement the bridemaids' gowns.

21. Buy wedding shoes and lingerie well before your wedding gown fitting. And break in those shoes!

22. Order note paper for your thank-you letters. If you have it monogrammed you must use your own initials until you are married, so don't overbuy unless you are retaining your maiden name.

23. Select bridemaids' dresses and headpieces. It is better not to shop en masse, because if you have six bridesmaids you are likely to have six different opinions. Discuss with them a satisfactory price range. Customarily they pay for their own outfits (see p. 53).

24. Notify your attendants to go to the store for measurements and to order their dresses.

25. The bride and groom should select and register their silver, china, and crystal. Seldom is a young man as domestically oriented as his bride-to-be, so to save confusion you might want to do some preliminary looking, then go together to make final decisions. (For monogramming, see p. 101.) List the stores in your file. Friends will often ask where you are listed, bless their hearts! (See p. 105.)

26. Remind everyone (grandparents, the groom and his family, and anyone else) that the deadline for their invitation lists is nearing.

27. Schedule time to shop for your going-away outfit and trousseau.

28. Set a date for house- or apartment-hunting. Set dates for furniture shopping. Make calendar notes.

29. Check on the bridesmaids. Have they ordered their dresses?

30. Make an appointment with your dentist for a checkup and any necessary work. Make a calendar note.

31. Order wedding invitations as soon as you have settled on the number of guests. Order a few extra; some will be spoiled in addressing (see p. 80).

32. While you are at the stationery store, order the bride's stationery trousseau: calling cards, informals, formal notes, everyday paper (see p. 99).

33. Meet bridesmaids to shop for shoes, which can all be dyed in one dye lot. Buy gloves if they are to be

worn. Gloves may be a welcome gift from the bride (see p. 54).

34. Select proper shade of pantyhose for bridesmaids, and have each girl buy a pair. Get an extra pair or two for emergencies.

35. For that little indiscernible extra that adds to the well-coordinated look, buy one shade of lipstick and nail polish for all your attendants to use.

36. When bridesmaids' dresses arrive at the store, notify your attendants to appear for fittings. Instruct fitter to correlate proper dress length for all attendants (see p. 55).

37. Have the invitations arrived? Perhaps you had better check. See page 85 for addressing instructions.

38. When the mother of the bride has selected her outfit, she can describe it to the groom's mother: length of dress, length of sleeves, color, and degree of formality. To create a harmonious picture in the receiving line, colors and styles should be coordinated. It is customary for the bride or her mother to suggest a selection of colors from which the groom's mother may choose. Black dresses are not suitable for this happy occasion.

39. At a home wedding:
    —The mothers do not wear hats or gloves.
    —If the wedding is limited to family and close friends, the mothers need not buy new dresses but may wear whatever is becoming and suitable for the time of day.
    —If a judge instead of a clergyman performs

the ceremony, suggest he wear his judicial robe for added dignity.

40. Rarely, but occasionally, it happens. The "it" refers to breaking an engagement or postponing the wedding date indefinitely. If you are contemplating such action, take time to discuss your problems, and do not confuse premarital jitters with a serious basic problem. If, after unemotional consideration, the wedding is canceled, you must take care of a few chores.

— If you have already mailed the invitations, you may send a printed card stating that by mutual consent the marriage will not take place. No further explanation is appropriate or necessary. If time is too short to notify the guests by mail, ask a few friends to organize a "telephoning committee."

— A similar newspaper announcement may be made. If your parents issued the previous announcement and invitations, they will also issue this "by mutual consent" cancellation announcement.

— Return all the wedding and shower gifts to the donors. Include a short, personal note along these lines: "Bob and I have agreed to cancel plans to marry. I am returning to you the beautiful salad bowl you sent us. Once again I thank you for your generosity and thoughtfulness."

— Cancel reservations and services.

— Privately admit to yourself, and enjoy the realization, that it is "better before than after."

— Put this book in a safe place to use later at a happier time.

Four to Six Weeks
Before the Wedding

The tempo begins to quicken. There are just a few more weeks before your wedding day. Look over your calendar to see if you need to make changes to uncrowd it. No reason for panic—just take one step at a time and all will be done.

41. Mail invitations four to six weeks ahead. Have the master list of guests' names ready to check off the number of acceptances. Early invitations mean early responses and early arrival of gifts—and more time for the bride's important thank-you notes. Reread page 8.

42. Arrange for fitting your bridal gown. Make a calendar note.

43. If the calendar is filling with party dates, you might like to send a schedule to your bridesmaids.

44. Make an appointment with your doctor for a complete physical checkup. Note date on calendar. If a blood test is required in your state, have it done at the same time as the physical.

45. Remind the groom to get his blood test if your state requires it.

46. Select groom's ring if it is to be a double-ring ceremony, and have it engraved. Now might be the time to select a gift for him. This is optional.

47. Select keepsake-type gifts for bridesmaids. Suitable gifts: earrings, a charm, any small piece of jewelry, a picture frame, a compact. The gift will become even more meaningful if it is engraved with the wedding date and the recipient's initials.

48. Remind the groom to select gifts for his ushers. These gifts should also be of the keepsake type. Refer him to page 130, item 5.

49. Set up a table for gift display. If the reception is to be held at home, you will want the gifts displayed at their best. In any event, you will want to invite interested, close friends to see your gifts (see p. 106).

50. Check your luggage. Have you the right cases for your honeymoon? Place them in your room early so you can begin preliminary packing as you think of what you will need.

51. To avoid any possible tendency to snap, how about a family champagne-tasting party now?

52. Obtain a floater policy to cover wedding gifts.

53. If you are assuming the groom's name, change it on insurance policies. Remind the groom to change the beneficiary on his life insurance policies.

54. Change the bride's name on her driver's license and legal papers.

55. Open bank accounts in new names.

56. Notify stores and credit card companies of the change of name, if applicable.

57. See your attorney about making a will.

58. Make an appointment for hair, manicure, and pedicure early in the week of the wedding. Note time on calendar. Try to avoid that just-out-of-the-beauty-shop look.

59. Order thank-you gifts or flowers for hostesses who entertain for you. Write thank-you notes the day after each party (see p. 48).

60. Some newspapers print wedding announcements; others do not. You must phone each paper you are interested in to learn its policy. Remember out-of-town papers if they apply to your situation (see p. 31 for more details).
Determine the following:
    —Will the newspaper send you a wedding form to fill out?
    —Does the paper want you to write your own release?
    —Will the paper print wedding pictures?
    —What is the deadline for submitting wedding information?
List the papers for the photographer, and tell him each newspaper's deadline for receiving the black-and-white glossies.

61. Plan housing arrangements for out-of-town attendants. This is your responsibility.

Consider the hazards of houseguests. The best-meaning and most beloved relatives and friends can be very wearing when you are busy and need to conserve your energy. Guests expect to be entertained, they are usually starving, and they might drain all the hot water in the house at a critical moment—just when the bride intended to shampoo her hair.

If friends offer to house your guests, accept gratefully. An alternative is to reserve rooms for all your out-of-town guests at the same hotel or motel, to simplify transportation.

For more pros and cons and solutions on the subject of houseguests, see page 109.

62. Bride's parents: think ahead to the time right after the wedding reception. Are there out-of-town guests, along with the wedding party, to be entertained? Make your plans now.

63. Will you need a parking service, an off-duty policeman, or other attendant, to direct parking at the reception? Engage whomever you need now, and arrange for payment before or after the wedding day.

64. Are you keeping the groom's family up to date with a duplicate guest list and a list of gifts you have received from their friends?

65. Arrange for someone to help the bride dress on the wedding day. Set the time for her to come to your home, and note it.

66. If you want to be completely extravagant and

pampered, have your hairdresser come to your home to comb your hair, and the bridesmaids' too. A delightful luxury.

67. Should you invite the officiating clergyman to the reception? Yes, if you are a member of his church, or if your parents or the groom's parents know him. If possible, the mother of the bride hand-delivers the engraved invitation, addressed to him and his wife. They are not expected to send a gift.

68. Go with the groom to get the marriage license. Note a convenient time on the calendar.

69. Invite your bridesmaids to a luncheon, or perhaps a dinner the same night as the bachelor dinner. Only your attendants need be present. This is an opportune time to give them their gifts and show them your trousseau and gifts.

70. Save some of the ribbons from gift and shower packages. Your bridesmaids can make them into mock bouquets to use at the wedding rehearsal.

71. A party is given before or after the rehearsal, usually the night before the wedding or sometimes two nights before. Do not stay out too late. Your list will include husbands and wives or fiancés of the members of the wedding party, and special out of town guests.

More and more frequently, the groom's parents host this party (see p. 150). However, if they do not offer, remember that it may be given by anyone, including the bride's family—away from their home, for the sake of their sanity.

72. Address and stamp announcements. They must be mailed *after* the wedding. Give them to a trustworthy friend to mail the day after the wedding. Then you can forget this detail.

73. If a bridesmaid or usher has to drop out at the last minute, do not attempt to find a replacement. The substitute might wonder why he or she was not invited in the first place.

Uneven numbers are quite acceptable in the processional and recessional—sometimes even by prearrangement. (This isn't Noah's Ark.)

74. Arrange a place for the bridesmaids to dress. This will avoid confusion when you want things to run smoothly. Tell them when they should come to your home for photographs and to be driven to the church.

75. If the wedding is scheduled for late afternoon or evening, it is not unusual for a close friend to entertain the members of the bridal party, parents, and out-of-town guests at a buffet lunch on the wedding day.

Even if you decide to follow the superstition of not seeing the groom until the ceremony, feel free to accept. One can leave before dessert; then it will be the other's turn. An "accomplice" can phone when the coast is clear.

This superstition stems from the past when marriages were arranged—complete with dowry—by fathers of the bride and groom. It was inadvisable for the groom to see his selected bride in case he didn't like her looks and bolted off!

76. Send reserved-pew cards to special guests and family members, or tell them to identify themselves to the ushers so they can be seated in front pews. Be certain

to take care of reserved pews for the groom's special guests too (see p. 113).

77. Select a responsible person to handle the guest book at the reception. This may be a youthful relative or a close friend who just missed being a bridesmaid. Plan to station her at a table ahead of the receiving line, but not too close. Provide two pens with the guest book when the time comes.

The guest book table can serve double duty if your reception plan includes a seated dinner or luncheon. On individual cards write the name and designated table number for each guest or couple. These small, imprinted cards and envelopes are available at stationery or bridal shops. Appoint someone to arrange them alphabetically on the table, ready to distribute when the guest book is signed.

78. You have probably thought of it a hundred times, but because this list tries to include everything, remember—you will need: someting old, something new, something borrowed, something blue, and a six-pence in your shoe. It is fun to understand the symbolism. The six-pence (or the shiny penny replacing it) denotes *prosperity* in your marriage. Blue denotes *faithfulness*. Borrowing shows *friendliness*. The old from your heritage combines with the new of your marriage into a *perfect union*.

79. Last reminder: Check the caterer, florist, photographer, musicians, hired drivers. Verify the delivery date of the wedding gown, the church arrangements, and the cake maker. A phone call to each can assure you all is in order.

The Last Week

Plan to slow down this week. If you have kept up faithfully with your thank-you notes, here is your well-earned reward: Relax now with a clear conscience. Aren't you glad you wrote all those notes? Any more from now on can wait until you return from your wedding trip.

80. Gather in one place everything you will need to dress for the wedding: gown, veil, underthings, pantyhose, cosmetics. Think. Then put everything together. Let there be no last-minute rushing about for stockings or a jar of cosmetics, or a last-gasp discovery that something you need has been packed.

You had better remind the groom to do the same.

81. Count acceptances for the reception and, unless you need an exact number for a sit-down dinner, estimate the number of late responders. Notify the caterer. A few people may bring uninvited children or friends. Prayer is the only defense against this.

82. Remind the groom to arrange for the best man to drive the getaway car or to order a car or taxi. The best man can hide the honeymoon car and help with hotel, train, or plane reservations.

83. Did anyone remember to fill all the cars with gasoline? This warning comes from memories of a wed-

ding delayed until the groom and best man finally arrived disheveled and out of breath. They had pushed the car with the empty gas tank the last two blocks!

84. Remind the maid of honor that it is her duty to inform the bride's parents and the groom's parents when the bride and groom are ready to leave after the reception. This is to allow a moment for good-byes.

85. Make sure the head usher understands about the reserved pews and passes the information along to the other ushers.

Give each usher a copy of the list of these special pew holders, in case some guests leave their cards at home (see p. 113).

86. *Hold those sprinklers!* If the reception will be in your garden, be sure the lawn is not watered for several days beforehand. Ladies totter perilously as their high heels sink into soft sod and ruin their shoes.

87. Pack suitcases for the honeymoon. Lay out everything to be packed; check and recheck. Put honeymoon luggage in the honeymoon car the night before the wedding—all except a cosmetic case.

88. Arrange your going-away handbag well ahead of time, while you are still thinking clearly.

89. You and your mother should read and reread the guest list to familiarize yourselves with the names. It will help when the receiving line forms.

90. Whoops! Let's not forget Father. He wants to

look his best. Remind him to get everything ready for the big day. Give him some help and a big kiss.

91. Arrange for a supply of sandwiches or snacks for the wedding party, photographers, dressers, and others who will be in your home on the wedding day.

92. If you are in doubt about how long it will take you to dress, have a "dress rehearsal" so there will be no rush on the wedding day.

93. Make up a little emergency kit—safety pins, needle and thread, facial tissue—for someone to take to the church.

94. Most important: Make out a time chart for the wedding day and tape it to your mirror. *Allow extra time all down the line*. If everything is done in slow motion, you will find that magically the *appearance of calmness* will actually make you *feel calm*.

95. Give your maid of honor the lipstick and nail polish for all the attendants to use.

96. Have a box of clean tissue paper ready for the ride to the church. Place the tissue under and around the bride's gown to keep it from mussing. Note to bride: Do not sit on your dress. Carefully place the train on the back of the car seat.

97. Board Fido and Kitty and all other pets on the day of the wedding. They do not belong.

98. It is the day of the wedding! A glorious day. Simply follow your time schedule. Bathe slowly.

Someone is coming to help you with your dress and veil. Everything is together and ready.

99. Take care with your makeup, which must last for several hours. Apply lipstick "permanently"; blot and powder between applications. Use an effective antiperspirant.

100. Use a light touch with your makeup. Do not try anything dramatically startling today.

101. Wear little or no jewelry with your wedding gown. Jewelry might detract from your own beauty— and every bride is beautiful.

102. You have taken care of all the details. There is nothing to be concerned about. Forget the mechanics now and make this a perfect day. Enjoy every moment and savor each one for the years to come.

Happy wedding!

Announcing Your Engagement

If you have not already announced your engagement, read on. Even if your engagement has been announced, save this section on teas, cocktail parties, and morning coffees to use after you settle into your new apartment or home. It will help when you entertain friends who entertained for you, and give you the opportunity to show some of your wedding gifts in use—not just on display. Later in your married life you will have many occasions to give simple or elaborate parties and will find these check lists handy.

Ways to Announce

Family First

As soon as you become engaged, your parents and your fiancé's parents must be the very first to know—before you breathe even a word to your best friend. If it is at all possible, tell both sets of parents in person.

If either of you plans to continue your education, you cannot blithely assume that your parents will be enchanted with the idea of subsidizing you. You had better find out how they feel about it. The size and cost of your wedding might depend upon the outcome of a frank talk about finances. Your parents might give you a choice between a lavish wedding or the money they would have spent on it.

It is customary for the groom's family to take the next step, which is to arrange a meeting with the bride's parents (see p. 146). The objective of such a meeting is to create a friendly and harmonious relationship. If, for some reason, the groom's parents do not take the first step in arranging a get-together, the bride's parents can graciously take the initiative.

Announcing to Friends

Take your choice:
—Simply call your best friends and let them spread the news. They will!
—A small family dinner. Your father or another relative will announce the engagement by proposing a toast to you and your fiancé.
—A tea.
—A cocktail party.

Mailed formal engagement announcements are not looked upon with favor. Instead, write a note to close interested friends who live elsewhere.

Newspaper Announcements

1. As stated earlier, newspapers have various policies. Refer to page 20, item 60, about wedding anouncements. The same applies to engagement announcements, namely that some papers do, and others do not, publish them. You will have to contact the papers you are interested in, to inquire about each one's policy. At the same time ask if they accept photographs; also obtain information about timing for later wedding submissions.

2. If your newspapers print this information, one news release will suffice provided you and your fiancé

are from the same town or city. If he and his parents live or have connections elsewhere, send those papers the item with a date "to be released . . ."

3. Traditionally your parents make the announcement. An engagement announcement starts with words to this effect:

> Mr. and Mrs. Douglas Andrew Blake of Pasadena, California, announced the engagement of their daughter, Sharon Anne, to Mr. Jeffrey Paul Fowler, Jr., the son of Mr. and Ms. Jeffrey Paul Fowler of Stamford, Connecticut. A December wedding is planned in Pasadena. . . .

The announcement continues with a brief résumé about the couple's schooling, occupation, wedding date, and future residence. A smaller hometown paper might like to include the names of the grandparents of longtime residents. One well-known newspaper publishes the names of former spouses, and even ages, for all the world to see.

You may compose your own announcement, or request an engagement form (and a wedding form to use later). This makes it easier to conform to each paper's individual style.

4. If one of the parents is no longer living, refer to him or her as "the late" Mr. or Mrs. in the body of the article. For example, "Mrs. Douglas Andrew Blake announces the engagement of her daughter, Sharon Anne, to . . ." etc. Then further into the release ". . . She is also the daughter of the late Mr. . . ."

NOTE: A second-time bride does not send an engagement announcement to the newspapers. A wedding announcement—yes (see p. 158).

AN ENGAGEMENT TEA

Although an engagement tea is similar to all tea parties, the decorations can be more sentimental and frilly, and the colors softer.

You attempt to surprise the guests, so think of an attractive way to divulge the news. Napkins and matchbook covers imprinted with the engaged couple's names are somewhat standard. Photographs or clever mantel or door decorations can tell the surprise. Use your ingenuity and originality.

1. At a small tea, one invites friends to come at a specified time. For a large tea, the invitations might state from three until five o'clock, four until six, or cover a three-hour period for a very large affair. Guests will come and go during those hours; however, count on the biggest crush about mid-time.

2. Occasionally a hostess considers staggering the hours on the invitation, inviting one group from two until three, another from three until four, and still another from four until five. *Resist this temptation.* Such regimentation defeats the purpose of a sociable afternoon. It is better to cut down the size of your guest list if necessary.

3. If yours is to be a large tea, plan on having a receiving line. Unless distance makes it impossible for the groom's mother to attend, she should be part of the

receiving line. The bride-to-be stands between her mother and her future mother-in-law.

4. In a receiving line it is easy to blank out and forget a name—even one's best friend—so don't worry if it happens. An advance review of the guest list usually helps, but fortunately a considerate guest will quickly give his name to jog your memory.

5. Ask a friend to assist—to greet, introduce, and direct guests toward the line.

6. When only a few people come to tea, the hostess pours, but for a formal tea, she honors several close relatives and friends by inviting them to pour for half- or three-quarter-hour periods.

7. The dining table is usually used for tea. Service for pouring tea and coffee is set at one or both ends, or at a separate table if space is at a premium. Remember sliced lemons, cream, sugar, and a pot of hot water.

8. Candles at teatime? Old rules decree no candles before five o'clock, but if the day is gloomy and wintry, who wouldn't prefer warm candle glow to the glare of incandescent bulbs?

9. Bite-size tea sandwiches, an assortment of cookies, candies, and nuts are arranged with artistic eye appeal. Stemmed strawberries are a luxury, but so pretty. If you decide to indulge, provide bowls of powdered and brown sugar, and sour cream for dipping.

10. Punch or iced tea is a refreshing addition to a summer tea.

11. The tea table should be as attractive and bountiful at the end of the day for late arrivals as it was at the start. Oversupply, and assign a friend or a waitress to keep the platters constantly replenished.

—Caterers count on five to six sandwiches per person, but in order to keep the platters filled, prepare more. A representative assortment will include four to six varieties.
—Add to the tea and coffee pots frequently, before they become lukewarm or empty.
—Have the used china taken to the kitchen immediately.

A SMALL TEA

Since it might be years into your married life before you have occasion to give a formal tea such as the engagement tea just outlined, here is a check list for a simplified informal tea you can use soon and often. Invite your bridesmaids, a neighbor or two, or congenial old or new friends.

Even if you have a hectic work schedule, you can find a few free minutes on a weekend, and after one or two of these relaxing teatime respites, you might just find this delightful formula habit-forming!

1. Assemble these basics for a small tea party:
—A tray with your best teapot or matching tea service
—Sugar bowl filled with cubes or colored crystals (not granulated sugar); sugar tongs or spoons
—Milk
—Lemon sliced thin, seedless; lemon fork

—Small napkins
—Spoons

2. Because it is difficult to juggle a cup, saucer, and separate plate, eliminate the saucer. Instead, use a dessert or salad-size plate with a matching cup. Tea sets are also available with off-center cup indentations, leaving room on the plate for sandwiches and cookies. Why not put these sets on your "want list."

3. Before guests arrive, preheat the teapot with hot water and put the kettle on to boil fresh water. It will take only a few moments away from your guests to steep the tea in the boiling water. Bring it in, seat yourself, pour and enjoy. Make coffee if you prefer.

4. What to serve:
   —You need serve only cookies, brownies, cinnamon toast, or other hot bread, such as wedges of toasted and buttered English muffins.
   —If you decide to make a few open-face sandwiches, then add something sweet—cookies, fruitcake, or candy.
   —As the number of guests increases, so will the selection on your tea table.

A MORNING COFFEE

Everything that applies to the format of a tea also fits the plan of a less-formal, morning coffee party, except the hours and the menu. You will still decorate the house with flower arrangements, and have a receiving line or not, as you wish.

Set the hours from ten until twelve o'clock, or nine-thirty until eleven-thirty.

Think of original ways to incorporate morning-type food into your menu: small ham sandwiches, eggs—devil them—sausages or chicken livers in a chafing dish, coffee cake, blueberry muffins, English muffins, dough-nut "holes."

A Cocktail Party

A cocktail party is another delightful way to announce your engagement, especially to introduce an out-of-town fiancé to friends.

Although everyone has attended dozens of cocktail parties, it is amazing how many questions you must answer, and decisions you must make, when you are about to give your own first party.

As at an announcement tea, the décor can tell the story, or your father or another relative can announce the news by proposing a toast to you and your fiancé.

Number of Guests

Decide how many guests you can accommodate comfortably without wall-to-wall people and intolerably high decibel levels. Depending upon the season of the year, perhaps you have a usable garden or deck to handle an overflow.

The Hours

A two-hour period is average, unless you plan to serve a light buffet and want guests to stay longer. Guests seldom arrive at the earliest time, so count on a mid-period crunch.

One More Decision Before You Invite

Substantial food or not?

At a cocktail party or open house, hors d'oeuvres alone are sufficient, and guests expect no more. You can serve make-ahead cold canapés or elaborate hot and cold varieties, depending upon whether you do it yourself or have help.

There are various ways to extend the menu, if you are so inclined, without becoming involved in a complete buffet dinner. If you decide to provide a light supper, be prepared to invite everyone to stay—VIP treatment for all or none.

Only after you complete your plan and are ready to be explicit can you send the invitations.

Inviting

Written invitations are timesavers for large parties, while inviting by telephone is advisable for small parties. Instant refusals will give you time to substitute other people. You may follow telephoned invitations with mailed reminder cards a week or ten days in advance, although reminders are used more often for dinners than for cocktails.

The reminder card is similar to the invitation diagrammed below. At the top of the card write the words, "To remind," and delete the R.s.v.p. You can use this same form when you host a party in honor of a friend. Just insert the words, "To honor (Sandra Smith)," either above or below the engraved names.

Fill-in cards come in almost unlimited variety. The slightly more formal engraved calling cards or French notes are convenient to use, especially if they already include the address.

Example

Mr. and Mrs. James Perry Standish

Cocktails
Friday, June 4 TH
6:00-8:30

75 Evergreen Drive
Danville, Kansas

R.S.V.P.

R.s.v.p. is also correct, even preferable.

"Regrets only" gives a sure clue to a large party. I prefer responses as insurance against invitations going astray—which they do with increasing frequency!

Seldom does one issue formal third-person invitations for cocktails, except for a reception.

Serving Drinks

If you have to choose between having a bartender *or* kitchen help, choose the bartender—professional or moonlighter. Kitchen work can be done ahead of time, whereas tending bar could consume a host's entire evening.

1. Provide the bartender with a jigger, and tell him exactly what strength drinks you wish him to pour.

Nothing can sabotage a party faster than a bartender with a heavy hand. To serve superstrong drinks is unkind to unsuspecting guests—even dangerous.

2. Set up one or more serving bars, or instruct waiters to circulate among the guests and take their orders.

3. At very informal gatherings the host can offer "courtesy of the bar," but his responsibility does not end there. He needs to check the bar often to replenish ice, soda, and other supplies, and he should encourage guests to pour their own drinks.

Stocking the Bar

For a work sheet for figuring quantities, and a list of drinks, including soft drinks and mixes, see the chart starting on page 184.

Start now to keep detailed records every time you entertain—even for another couple. You might wonder what value these records have, but you will find that a hostess book will serve you well time and time again—almost like having an extra brain! Record the guests' names, menu, table arrangements, flowers, and shopping lists. The following day, add your personal comments that would make the next time easier or better. Hospitality and easy entertaining, aided by your records, will make your friends' lives and your own more pleasant.

Save these outlines to use later. For now—on with wedding planning. . . .

Church Arrangements

Name of clergyman _____ Phone _____

Correct, full name of church _____

_____

Address _____ Phone _____

Day _____ Date _____ Hour _____

Clergyman's secretary _____ Phone _____

Times for premarital conferences _____

Time and date for rehearsal _____

Time to arrive at church on wedding day _____

Descriptions of the rituals and requirements of various denominations have been intentionally omitted from this book. You will either already know the necessary specifics that apply to *your* ceremony, or you will learn about them from the clergyman or his secretary.

The bride and groom's prime priority is an early first conference with the clergyman of his or her church.

If neither one has a church affiliation, don't set your heart on your wedding taking place in one particular church until after you confer. Even within the same denomination one finds clergymen with differing attitudes, interpretations, and regulations. For this reason all your wedding plans will depend upon *who* will officiate— and *where*.

BRIDE AND GROOM DISCUSS WITH THE CLERGYMAN:

1. Do you need to obtain a dispensation, or permission to marry, in case of divorce or mixed marriages? Are marriages permitted on Sunday? During Lent? Any restrictions regarding attendants' religions?

2. Does the church require premarital conferences, or attendance over a period of time, before your marriage?

3. If you and your husband-to-be are of different faiths, you may want to ask if a clergyman representing each of your faiths may officiate jointly. They often do.

4. Can you obtain approval if you wish to incorporate special or personally written vows? Not all clergymen will consent.

5. Ascertain the form and length of the service.

6. Secure permission from the clergyman or his secretary for soloist, choir, other music of your choice, or guest-singing participation.

7. Some couples memorize their vows and speak them instead of repeating the clergyman's statements.

"Speaking" is delightful only when done easily; it is painful to hear when, under tension, the vows come out whispered, or garbled. Unless you are confident you will both—repeat *both*—be comfortable and relaxed, stay with the conventional exchange of vows. They are lovely.

8. The groom can find information about the clergyman's fee on page 132, item 15. This is the groom's responsibility.

THE BRIDE'S ARRANGEMENTS

All but the smallest of churches will have a secretary, and in addition many will have a wedding coordinator. Either one is well versed in everything that takes place within the church and will advise you on all the following details, the order of the procession and recession, and more.

9. Payment for sexton. Payment for organist if provided by the church. Other charges.

10. Are any specific musical numbers banned?

11. Rules regarding photography and video recording inside the church.

12. Facilities for the bridal party to freshen up, or to dress if they have to drive a great distance.

13. Where the bridal party should park.

14. Decorations. Any restrictions regarding flowers or candles?

15. Ask if a wedding is scheduled immediately before or after yours. Sometimes the secretary or church wedding coordinator will put the two brides in touch, so they may cooperate in planning and sharing the cost of flowers.

16. Does the church provide a kneeling cushion?

17. Some churches provide a community room in which to hold a reception. If you are interested, check on the details (see p. 128, item 2).

18. Reread item 67, page 22. It refers to inviting the clergyman and his wife to the reception.

19. If you are acquainted with the wedding coordinator of your church, she will appreciate an invitation to the reception.

Showers

Lucky you! How generous and thoughtful of friends to plan a shower for you! Note the word *friends*—never a close member of either your family or the groom's family. Such an invitation from a family member might appear to solicit gifts—no matter how innocent their intentions—and that would never do. If a close relative wishes to honor you, then a luncheon, tea, cocktail party, or dinner would be delightful.

Unless the shower hostess plans to surprise you, which is risky business, she will discuss plans with you. Besides setting the date, she will ask you to make up a guest list, and will probably consult you on the kind of shower and the colors you prefer.

GUEST LISTS

1. Before you make your list, ask the hostess how many she would like to entertain. Insist on a specific number, then make your list accordingly, allowing for a few refusals.

2. It is inadvisable to include the same people at more than one shower.

3. Include only those friends you intend to invite to the wedding and reception.

4. Even if your future mother-in-law lives out of town, place her name on the lists for courtesy invitations. She will enjoy keeping up to date with your activities.

5. Have compassion for your bridesmaids' already strained budgets. Select a low-cost category when they will be among the guests, and whisper that old cliché—that you desire their presence, not their presents.

KINDS OF SHOWERS

Before you settle on a category, consider the following list of possibilities—a few of which include the men. The comments about them might help you decide. Best are those that allow donors to select from a wide price range.

Spare yourself from criticism for asking for anything as mercenary as a "money tree"!

1. Kitchen. Good because of the wide price range, from a pot holder to a set of knives. Specify color preferences.

2. Bathroom. Specify color preferences.

3. Recipes and ingredients. Anything from a special herb to an appropriate mold or cooking utensil. Need not be expensive.

4. Pantry—extravagant gourmet or essential and practical.

5. Paper goods. Numerous innovative ideas.

6. Round-the-clock. The invitation assigns each

guest an hour of the day or night. The guest selects a gift suitable for that hour. The honoree may open the gifts in order of time, perhaps starting with an alarm clock, then a bath towel or box of soap, next a coffeepot or jam jar. This is the most fun!

7. A room shower is similar to the round-the-clock shower. Instead of assigning times, you specify a certain room, such as the guest room, powder room, kitchen, or breakfast room. Obviously, this is inappropriate if the couple will be moving into a three-room apartment.

8. Closet accessories. The hostess will have to coordinate this one so everything will match.

9. Pots and pans. Almost too expensive a category for individual donors unless they pool their resources.

10. Linens. Expensive unless two or more guests give jointly.

11. Lingerie. Consider this as a trousseau item.

12. Crystal or china. These come under the wedding-gift category.

13. Miscellaneous. More difficult for the donor, and not as much fun for the recipient.

Sometimes a groom feels left out of prewedding festivities, but he won't if you suggest an evening shower with gifts for him:

14. Household tools. Anything from thumbtacks or a measuring tape to a step stool.

15. Gadgets. A remarkable variety!

16. House plants and related accessories, if they fit your life-style and will not have to be transported too far. Planting supplies, pebbles, containers, macramé hangers, etc.

17. Gardening tools and supplies—if you will be moving into a home.

18. Gourmet cooking items, now that many men are showing an interest and flair.

19. Bar equipment. Towels, openers, jiggers, even wine and liqueurs.

20. For his interest or hobby. Music? Fishing? Sports? Photography?

At a shower be certain someone is listing each gift and its donor. It is almost impossible to pair gifts with cards later. Ask another helper to retrieve the ribbons and create a "bouquet" to use at the rehearsal.

Each gift has merit, so always thank the giver profusely.

Guests enjoy handling the gifts. Instead of holding gifts up to view across the room, start each box on a tour of the circle.

A GIFT FOR THE HOSTESS

Send your hostess a gift after the shower or a flower arrangement to use at the party. If you plan to send flowers, tell her in advance, and spare her unnecessary effort and expense. Inquire about her color scheme and where she would like to place the arrangement.

GOOD ADVICE

Should you report parties given for you to the newspapers? Not without your hostess' permission. To do so could spark the end of a beautiful friendship if she dislikes publicity.

ONE LAST DECISION

Should you write thank-you notes even though you have thanked the donors at the party?

Yes!

A little efficiency tip from my well-organized daughter: Having known the guest list in advance, she addressed and stamped envelopes ahead of time. After the shower, with half the work already done, she was able to concentrate on brief, enthusiastic notes. She warns, however, to be careful not to mail the empty envelopes *before* the party takes place!

If a wedding gift arrives from one of the shower guests before you have had a chance to write, you may combine your thanks for both presents into one letter.

Wedding Gown and Veil

FINAL SELECTION

Store _____ Phone _____

Salesperson _____ Extension _____

Fitting appointments _____

Date of delivery _____

You will find that selecting a wedding gown is one of the most exciting aspects of wedding planning—and, understandably, a happy tear-jerker for your mother if she shops with you.

Now that tradition is undeniably back in high favor, wedding gowns are more beautiful than ever—all so lovely that it is difficult to choose just a single one.

Along with the return to tradition, it naturally follows that many brides love the sentiment of wearing the gowns worn by their mothers, aunts, or sisters. If the gown was "heirloomed" (see p. 156, item 5), you already have a big advantage; however, if it has slightly yellowed, call it "ivory."

Expert designers have both the vision and expertise to transform a size six gown into a size ten, and then challenge you to find the alteration points.

A lace veil previously worn by another might not be becoming in its original state, but it, too, can be skillfully redesigned to flatter and delight you.

1. Allow at least four to six months if your gown has to be ordered, then fitted.

2. Gowns range in price from moderate to enormous. Before you shop, decide how much you can comfortably spend.

3. Choose a wedding gown that is appropriate for the time of day, and consistent with the formality or informality of your overall plan:

    —Formal daytime or evening: long gown; short or long train; long, fingertip, or short veil.
    —Summer garden: lighter weight fabric without a train.
    —Informal morning: suit, or street-length dress with or without a jacket; no veil; hat optional.
    —Informal evening: long or short "cocktail dress."

4. Gloves: If your gown has long sleeves, there is no need for gloves. With a short-sleeved or sleeveless dress, consider:

    —Short gloves a half-size larger than you usually wear, so you can slip off the left glove and give it to the maid of honor to hold.

—Fingerless mitts.

—Long white gloves that you will not remove. Either roll back to the wrist, or have the store rip the seams of the ring finger.

— You will wear your engagement ring on your right hand the day of the wedding, so the wedding ring can properly be placed first on your finger.

5. At a small home wedding:

—Gloves are inappropriate.

—A short or long dress, in white or a soft color, with or without a short veil, is suitable.

—If the wedding is limited to family and a few close friends, you may prefer to be married in your going-away suit without a veil.

6. Buy the wedding shoes and underthings before the fitting. Remember to break in the shoes.

7. After you've had your gown fitted, don't impulsively go on a crash diet. You might discover too late that although you shrank, your gown didn't.

8. If your budget won't stretch as far as you would like, investigate other alternatives:

—Ready-to-wear gowns.

—End-of-season sales.

—If you can step into a sample model, occasionally you can buy the sample for less than the same style if you ordered it.

—Discount outlets.

—Rented gowns at less than half their original retail cost.

—Some rental shops buy only from the bridal gown manufacturers. Others will buy once-used gowns to add to their rental inventory. This option will require diligent research on your part.

Happy Hunting!

Bridesmaids' Gowns

Remember that a popular girl's closet might already be filled with dressy, unwearable gowns from previous bridesmaid stints. Try to find dresses they "can't wait to wear again," or can have remodeled later. Selecting dresses in a color and style to fit assorted sizes, shapes, coloring, and tastes is not an easy assignment, but with patient effort, you can accomplish wonders.

In addition to choosing a color that is becoming to your attendants, visualize it in the church and reception settings. For example, shell pink might look enchanting in a light and airy church, while stronger jewel tones would complement cathedral architecture. If you are in doubt, take a color sample and judge it in the settings where it will be worn.

If the bridemaids are scattered, have their dresses delivered to them in time to have any needed alterations.

Bridesmaids customarily pay for their own outfits. Here are two possible budget stretchers for them:

— Their dresses can be made to your specifications at home, or by a dressmaker.
— You can shop for rental bridesmaids dresses. It is even more difficult to find rentals for bridesmaids than for brides, but perhaps your perseverance will be rewarded.

One further thought about the cost of bridesmaids gowns. If the entire wedding is lavish, and the selected dresses wildly expensive, the bride's parents may pay for them—while rationalizing that the gowns are part of the "wedding decor." A fantasy solution!

FINAL SELECTION

Store _____ Phone _____

Salesperson _____ Extension _____

BRIDESMAID _____ BRIDESMAID _____

Size pantyhose _____ Size pantyhose _____

Size dress _____ Size dress _____

Size gloves _____ Size gloves _____

BRIDESMAID _____ BRIDESMAID _____

Size pantyhose _____ Size pantyhose _____

Size dress _____ Size dress _____

Size gloves _____ Size gloves _____

BRIDESMAID _____ BRIDESMAID _____

Size pantyhose _____ Size pantyhose _____

Size dress _____ Size dress _____

Size gloves _____ Size gloves _____

1. Select hats or headpieces, or order fresh flower hair adornments from the florist.

2. If you have invited a junior bridesmaid or flower girl, select a harmonizing dress suitable for her age.

3. Ask the fitter to correlate the lengths of the bridesmaids' dresses.

4. Take a dress sample when you purchase lipsticks and nail polish.

5. Reread and follow items 23 and 24 on page 14.

6. Jewelry: Preferably bridesmaids should not wear watches or bracelets. Simple earrings and perhaps a delicate necklace are enough.

To simplify and clarify, send each bridesmaid a schedule of the wedding week. Include:
- —Reminder to break in new shoes
- —List of parties
- —Rehearsal time and place
- —Rehearsal dinner time and place
- —Where bridesmaids will lunch or dine or have tea before wedding
- —Where bridesmaids will dress
- —Time and place for prewedding photographs
- —Pairing with ushers for the drive from the church to the reception, and ". . . please come quickly so the receiving line won't be held up . . ."

Bridal Consultants

You might ask, "Do I need a consultant?" That depends solely upon you, your temperament, your schedule and pressures, your parents, or lack of parental help.

Most couples prefer to go through the process of investigating on their own and then, with this book to guide them, attend to the many details themselves. When they make their personal choices, they feel they have achieved a wedding uniquely their own.

There are situations, however, in which a competent consultant or coordinator is not only a boon but a necessity. Engaging the right one for *you* becomes a very personal choice, because you will work together closely and must "click." There can be no opposing goals or ideas.

The following considerations should help you in your selection:

WHAT CAN A CONSULTANT OR COORDINATOR DO FOR YOU?

The terms are used interchangeably here, although each seems to have its own interpretation. Some consultants will take *full charge* of everything from start to finish; others will assist to a *limited degree* in the particular areas you specify.

Full Charge

An expert full-charge consultant can personally direct the logistics and take responsibility for every phase of the preparations, including the important wedding day itself.

> —She has often encountered and solved the same problems that are new and worrisome to you.
>
> —She will know which of the many caterers, photographers, bakers, florists, and other services are dependable and efficient, and will engage them.
>
> —She will even take charge of ordering, addressing, and sending invitations and announcements.
>
> —Should you need a reception location, she can provide a list that includes cost of rental, capacity, available equipment, parking facilities, and liquor restrictions. She will make arrangements for the one you select.
>
> —Most self-employed consultants have imagination and a flair for entertaining. Only you can judge whether you are on the same wavelength.

Limited Assistance

1. Some coordinators are primarily caterers who have expanded their contacts in order to fulfill their clients' other requirements. They will have available dishes, silver, chafing dishes, and other serving needs. They should be able to oversee the reception routine.

Just as restaurants vary in quality and expertise, so do caterer/consultants.

2. Major stores and some bridal shops provide consultants who coordinate the wedding party gowns, including that of the mother-of-the bride.

> —They will help the bride select and register gifts from the store's selection. They will have helpful suggestions based on their experiences with many brides.
>
> —Occasionally they will deliver the gown on the wedding day and help the bride dress.
>
> —A store consultant rarely handles all the services you will need.

WHAT WILL IT COST?

Before that question can be answered, you must be aware of how diverse these services are.

One coordinator might specialize in the-sky's-the-limit elegance, while another takes pride in her economy, even to making available rental wedding gowns. That is why it is essential that you discuss your financial limits frankly. If one consultant is not able to produce what you want within your allotment, consult another.

Charges are made in a variety of ways:

> —A flat fee. Inquire exactly what the fee includes and omits.
>
> —A percentage, ranging from ten percent up to forty percent, is added onto the bills for services, in which case she will submit the bills to you.
>
> —A fee plus a commission paid directly from the various suppliers they engage.
>
> —An in-house consultant is paid by the establishment for whom she works.

A LUXURY OR A NEED?

Interview the consultants in depth before you select one with whom you can work congenially. If possible, talk to people who have used the services of the one you are considering. Were they satisfied?

After you've done your homework, you will know if a consultant is for you.

Caterer

Name _____ Phone _____

Address _____

Your first questions after reading the chapter title will probably be, "Do we really need a caterer? What can a caterer do that we can't do by ourselves or by hiring extra help?"

Whether or not you use a caterer depends upon you. If your reception is to be held in a hotel or club, the catering department will provide all the necessities, but if the reception is at home or in a rented hall, you will have to make your own arrangements for food and service.

The factors to consider are the number of guests, time of day, location, customs of your community, and expense. You will be ready to make your decision after you read the following information.

WHAT A CATERER CAN PROVIDE

1. A competent caterer will provide the food and an adequate staff of cooks, waiters or waitresses, and bartenders. He prepares much of the food in his own

kitchen. If one's own kitchen facilities are limited, he can transport hot food in portable ovens.

2. He can supply glasses, dishes, tea service, punch bowls, tables, tablecloths, chairs—almost everything you want.

3. Caterers are experienced in what they call "circulation" for serving, and in receiving-line procedure. Discuss your reception with him in detail. He is responsible for a multitude of parties, so take advantage of his knowledge. He might be able to suggest a previously unthought of location for the receiving line to relieve congestion.

There is no law that says the bride *must* receive in front of the fireplace—especially if that position would hamper circulation. Variations are almost unlimited.

> —Set up a tent. Portable heaters can do wonders for a tented area.
> —Transform a two-car garage into a temporary party room and receive there. Yes, a garage! You have only to remove bicycles, paint cans, and other clutter, and start decorating. Cover the floor with a borrowed or rented rug; for tables, set up sawhorses topped with planks or a door and cover them with pretty cloths or satin yardage; rent espalliered trees or shrubs for a beautiful background.
> —You might decide to have some of the furniture removed from the house and held overnight in a moving van. This would enable you to use floor space freely. Dance in the dining room and dine in the living room.

4. Some caterers are qualified to handle the decorating and arrange for music, flowers, and other special services if you wish.

5. Some caterers can act as majordomo, or they can offer the services of a hostess who will keep the reception routine flowing smoothly.

HOW TO DECIDE ON THE BEST CATERER

Depend heavily upon strong recommendations from people whose style you admire and respect. Rarely—but occasionally—one hears of a caterer who underestimated quantity and ran out of food with fifty guests yet to be served. Horrible thought!

HOW A CATERER CHARGES

A catering firm will arrive at the total charge by adding together the following items and submitting a contract for you to sign.

$ . . . Either the total cost of food plus an agreed-upon percentage *or*, more often, the cost of each serving or dinner multiplied by the number of guests—known as the charge per head. Your menu choices will govern the cost.

$ . . . Charges for the staff's working time.

$ . . . Dishes, glasses, and other equipment you request.

$ . . . Other specified services or provisions, such as music, decorations, drinks, wedding cake.

———

$$ . . Total

The caterer will estimate from his own experience the number of waiters or waitresses he needs for your reception. To assure excellent service, I always ask the caterer to engage an extra two persons to help. A bit extravagant, but you might decide it is worth the extra—just this once!

At the original consultation you can roughly estimate the number of guests. The contract will state a cut-off date for specifying a firm number.

Most caterers will submit a bill after the reception takes place. Pay him promptly. Some caterers will request a sizable advance payment; others ask for full payment in advance. I would never engage the latter caterer.

CANCELING A CONTRACT

If, due to an emergency, you have to call off or postpone the wedding, what is your obligation? A contract is an agreement to pay regardless of personal problems. However, if you cancel far enough ahead, you might be granted some leniency.

Leniency depends upon the caterer's attitude and often on his relationship with a customer. If you are a good customer, he will probably take that into consideration. If it is too late to place the staff elsewhere, you will be fully obligated to pay. If he has not yet purchased the food, he might relieve you of that expense.

Caterers who are also in the restaurant business are often able to use the food, even if you cancel late; if they cannot use it, they will charge you.

ITEMS TO CHECK

Whether you engage a caterer, hire your own help, or use the assistance of kind friends, you will need to make decisions about all the following items. Cross off the items that do not apply to your plan.

1. Who will furnish the wedding cake? Prices, workmanship, quality, and taste vary considerably. In addition to the kind of cake, size, and cost, discuss:

  —Decoration. Consider substituting flowers made of icing for the little bride-and-groom figures so often seen atop cakes. Better still are real flowers in a tiny glass set into the top of the cake. Look up nonpoisonous varieties of flowers. Fresh flowers can also be used spilling out between the cake tiers. Sparkling crystal decorations, while ruinous to your bankbook, are exquisite to behold.

  —Fruitcake for the top tier, called the groom's cake, can be saved to enjoy on your first anniversary.

  —Boxed individual slices of wedding cake. These are an unexpected and unnecessary luxury today.

2. Napkins. Do you want them printed with the bride's and groom's names or initials?

3. Match booklets. Do you want them printed with names or initials? The date?

4. Coat racks, if needed. If so, you'll need coat hangers too.

5. Tables and chairs.

6. Glasses.

7. Dishes.

8. Punch bowl.

9. Silver.

10. Menu. Is there to be a formal, seated bride's table? Read reception notes starting on page 123.

11. Beverages. An open bar?

12. Tubs to ice champagne. You can chill large quantities in the tub of your washing machine. Afterward simply drain or spin out the melted ice, or add water and detergent to soak dish towels and napkins.

13. Serving centers must be located.

14. Location of wedding cake table.

15. Guest book table.

16. Rice, confetti, or rose petals to be passed before couple leaves (see note p. 127).

17. Ice.

18. Station help at the door to take wraps, in the gift-display room, and to pass refreshments. Review the chapter on the reception to remind yourself where you will need service.

19. Who will move furniture before and after the reception?

20. An alternate plan in case of rain—if you are planning a garden wedding.

21. Depending upon the couple's destination, you might ask the caterer to place a festive box lunch in the getaway car. Include sandwiches, champagne, glasses, and, of course, slices of your wedding cake.

EXTRA HELP

Name _____ Phone _____

Name _____ Phone _____

Name _____ Phone _____

Photographs and Videotapes

Name _____ Phone _____

Address _____

Time of Arrival _____

Name _____ Phone _____

Address _____

Time of Arrival _____

The permanent record of your ceremony and reception is next in importance to the wedding itself. You will look at the photographs or watch the videotapes over and over again during your lifetime. Start the tradition of viewing your pictures on each anniversary date. It is almost like renewing your vows.

Brides are often surprised and distressed to find that the photographer of their choice was booked months ago, and they must settle for fourth or fifth choice. Investigate, then engage your photographer or video service (or both) as soon as you possibly can.

1. Engage a photographer who is a specialist in weddings. An excellent portrait photographer is not necessarily adept at handling group pictures or candid shots

discreetly. A specialist is familiar with wedding procedure and timing. He will anticipate the bridal couple's
next move and will be in the proper place at the proper
time.

2. A clear understanding of what the photographer
will do is essential.
> —Ask your friends for their recommendations.
> —Ask to see a photographer's finished work be-
> fore you make a final decision.
> —Make sure *you* can select the pictures for the
> albums.
> —Be certain you will have a sufficient number
> of proofs to allow an adequate selection.
> —Make certain the photographer will take all
> the special pictures you request.
> —The fee is partially based upon the time re-
> quired. To avoid misunderstandings and con-
> sequent disappointment, specify enough time
> for him to stay throughout the reception.
> —Get a firm price *in writing* on pictures and
> albums. How many pictures will be included
> in the album?
> —What is the cost of extra prints? Extra albums
> for parents?
> —Does the photographer require a down pay-
> ment? Will he submit the proofs and deliver
> the finished photographs before you make the
> final payment?
> —When will the proofs be submitted? When can
> you expect the finished photographs?
> —Will he object to candid shots snapped by
> enthusiastic friends? He should not object; the
> candids will not replace his work.

3. When you are in complete agreement, make it clear you wish to engage the photographer whose portfolios you like, not the studio. Request "no substitute."

4. Arrange a time and place for your formal bridal portrait if you desire one. Some fine gown salons provide space for this at the time of the final fitting. Consider these advantages of having your portrait taken on the wedding day:
  —The wedding bouquet will be your own.
  —Your gown will not have to be transported to a studio.
  —A bride is *always* most beautiful on her wedding day.

5. Give the photographer a list of pictures you must have. In addition to the standard high points, such as cutting the cake and toasting, you will want a picture of the groom's parents with the bride and groom, the girl with the guest book, and candids of certain relatives and friends. You will ask a responsible person to stay with him long enough to point out those people.

6. Arrange to have as many pictures as possible taken before the wedding: the bride with her bridesmaids; the bride with her father, her mother, the whole family.

7. Videotaping of weddings is increasingly popular. As with photographers, one can find all levels of expertise and service. Investigate thoroughly to assure getting exactly what you want.

You might put a video player on your "most wanted" gift list.

A qualified video recording organization can provide anything from an unedited ceremony-only tape, produced by a single camera, to the ultimate of a highly edited day-long production with two or more cameras in action. You will also find a number of variations between these two extremes. The price scale ranges accordingly.

Reread the items to discuss with the photographer, much of which applies to videotaping.

At present the quality of pictures printed from videotape is not satisfactory. With the wondrous advancements in technology, we can look forward to pictures printed from tapes someday—maybe even by the time you use this book.

8. Set the exact time for the photographer or videotaper to be at the church, but first ascertain the church's rules regarding picture-taking. Some churches forbid it; others specify which studios they favor—based upon the photographers' previous restrained manners.

If church pictures are permitted, remind the photographers and videotapers to be discreet—no dashing down the aisle in pursuit of a picture . . . and never, *never* permit a camera in the chancel, on the rail, or near the altar. No matter how much you might like a photograph from that angle, it is not worth spoiling the beauty and solemnity of your perfect wedding.

Some clubs and hotels also have rules and restrictions about videotaping because of the need to set up cables and lighting. Permission must be obtained *in advance* from the Board of Directors or the Manager.

9. Most professionals—both men and women— will wear clothes that blend with the guests' attire. Once in a while, however, a man will appear to take pictures wearing a flamboyant shirt without a tie or jacket;

a woman might wear something equally inappropriate for a formal wedding. A discordant note, indeed! Try to cover this point tactfully in advance.

A photographer may certainly give a guest his business card, if requested, but should never display advertising, even on his lapel.

10. Instruct the photographer not to hold up the receiving line by taking too many pictures while guests are waiting. He has heard this many, many times. Tell him again, and mean it.

11. Give the photographer a written list of newspapers to which he should send your favorite glossy prints. Send different poses if the newspapers are located in towns close to each other.

12. Suggest that the best photographers are invisible. He may rebel, but remember, it is *your* wedding.

13. Sometimes a nonprofessional friend will offer to record your day on film. He might plan to make this your wedding present—and a fine one indeed! If you accept his generosity, supply him with film, and give him an important gift afterward. For a large wedding, however, a nonprofessional photographer would not be as satisfactory. You would be reluctant to give a friend who donates his services the same directions you would give a person you pay.

Florist

Name _____ Phone _____

Address _____

Tuck this book into your handbag when you consult the florist, and discuss all the points listed below. Although the groom will pay for some of the flowers (see p. 132, item 14), he will usually ask you to make the selections and have the bill sent to him.

1. Church decoration. After the ceremony the florist can transport the flowers from the church and add them to the reception decorations. A further thought: If another wedding is scheduled to precede or follow yours in the church, you might investigate sharing the cost, provided your tastes are similar.

2. Reception decorations.

3. Decoration for the wedding-cake table. If you want the cake decorated with fresh flowers, see page 64, item 1.

4. White satin ribbons and flowers for the cake knife.

5. Small flowers tied with white ribbon on stems of champagne toasting glasses.

6. Bride's bouquet. Discuss what will be suitable with the gown. Proportion is important. Some brides choose to carry a white prayer book without flowers, or with a marker of satin ribbon and flowers.

7. Bride's going-away corsage, if desired.

8. Corsages for the bride's mother and groom's mother to wear or to pin to their handbags.

9. Boutonnieres for ushers, best man, groom, and fathers.

10. Flowers for the bride's attendants. Costly varieties of flowers are less important than styling, proportion, and color.

11. Time and place of delivery:
    a. Bridal party _____

    _____
    (in time for photographs)
    b. Mothers' corsages _____

    _____
    c. Boutonnieres for the men _____

    _____
    d. Grandmothers' corsages _____

    _____

12. Most florists can provide a canvas runner for the center aisle if you desire one.

If you intend to do your own decorating, don't leave it until the wedding day.

There is a popular misconception that the term "fresh flowers" means they are arranged immediately after they are cut. According to the experts, flowers and greenery are fresher and last longer after they have been hardened.

To harden: Strip the stems of all leaves that will be in the water; submerge the stem ends and cut to the desired length under water. This method will prevent air pockets from forming and will encourage the intake of water.

Soak greenery in deep water for at least a day; soak flowers for at least several hours after you make the new cut. Keep in a cool place.

NOTE: The groom customarily pays for the bride's bouquet, corsages for the mothers, and boutonnieres for the ushers, best man, and himself. He *may* pay for the attendants' flowers.

Music for the Church

Organist _____ Phone _____

Address _____

Soloist _____ Phone _____

Address _____

Other Musicians _____ Phone _____

Address _____

1. You will have determined at your church conference if you are required to use a church-provided
organist (whom you will pay), or if you may engage
outside musicians.

You have also been informed if certain musical
numbers are not permitted.

2. The best scheduling for a choir, soloist, or other
special music is immediately before the processional if
the ceremony is short, or while a Communion is being
prepared if the ceremony is long.

3. Make certain the musicians know the selections
you request.

4. Arrange to pay before or after the wedding day.

Musicians for the Reception

Name _____ Phone _____

Address _____

1. There need be no music at all at the reception. If you want music, however, it can be anything from one piece—a piano, accordion, or zither—to two dance bands.

2. Decide what the musicians will wear.

3. Set an exact time for the musicians' arrival at the reception.

4. Arrange for a special fanfare to announce the cake cutting.

5. Well in advance, give the leader a list of the bride's and groom's favorite selections for both background and dance music.

6. If there is to be no dancing, the musicians will play background music only.

7. If there is to be dancing, the musicians will play background music until the dancing begins. No one may

dance until the bride and groom have had their first dance. The dancing sequence goes like this:

First dance: bride and groom alone.

Second dance: bride and her father; groom and bride's mother.

Third dance: bride and groom; bride's father and groom's mother; bride's mother and groom's father; ushers and bridesmaids. Then all dance. Anyone may cut in and dance with the bride. Guests love it.

Drivers

Hire limousines, or arrange for willing friends to drive. Give precise instructions in either case, whether to professionals or friends.

1. Bride to church, accompanied traditionally by her father:

Driver _____ Phone _____

2. Bridesmaids to church and return for the reception:

Driver _____ Phone _____

Driver _____ Phone _____

Driver _____ Phone _____

Time to report at house _____

3. Bride's mother, unless she rides with bride or bridesmaids:

Driver _____ Phone _____

Time to report _____

4. Grandparents or others:

Driver _____ Phone _____

Time _____ Place _____

5. Groom's parents:

Driver _____ Phone _____

Time _____ Place _____

6. Has everyone been provided with the following?
—Information on where to pick up each passenger.
—Exact times for pickups.
—Estimated time to travel to destination. (Allow a little latitude when estimating the timing.)
—A map, if it would prove useful.

7. Did you arrange for the groom's parents to return promptly from the church so the receiving line can start without delay?

8. Bridesmaids may return from the church with the ushers—if they promise to return promptly.

9. If you hire drivers, arrange to pay them either before or after the wedding day.

Invitations, Announcements, and Addressing

If you appreciate the elegance of traditional invitations—which will set the tone of your wedding—go to a reputable, established stationer. The very best stationers with experienced personnel charge no more than other stores that might prove unsatisfactory.

Qualified people can advise you on the proper and current styles of lettering, size and quality of paper, and the correct wording for church or home weddings and announcements. They are prepared to give you information about reception cards, map enclosures when needed, and At Home cards, which are enclosed only in announcements.

You might have a special situation—unusual to you but totally familiar to experienced stationers. Their understanding, good taste, and knowledge of etiquette can guide you. Second-time brides will find their special information in the chapter starting on page 158.

A few examples of conventional wedding invitations are included. Those who admire and respect tradition will be interested to know that, according to very old etiquette books, the style, format, and every word remain unchanged.

A Traditional Church Wedding Invitation
Mr. and Mrs. Douglas Andrew Blake
request the honour of your presence
at the marriage of their daughter
Sharon Anne
to
Mr. Jeffrey Paul Fowler, Jr.
Date
Time
Church name
Church address (if needed)

A Wedding Not in a Church
Mr. and Mrs. Douglas Andrew Blake
request the pleasure of your company
etc.

A Divorced Mother
Mrs. Barbara Guest or Mrs. Townsend Guest—
whichever form you customarily use. (See page 86,
item E.)

If the Bride's Mother Has Remarried
Mr. and Mrs. Howard Thomas Whiting
request the honour of your presence
at the marriage of her daughter
Sharon Anne Blake
etc.

A Bride and Groom on Their Own at a Church
The honour of your presence
is requested at the marriage of
Miss Sharon Anne Blake
to
Mr. Jeffrey Paul Fowler, Jr.
etc.

Or Other Than a Church

Miss Sharon Anne Blake
and
Mr. Jeffrey Paul Fowler, Jr.
request the pleasure of your company
at their marriage
etc.

Announcements follow the pattern of the invitations:

Mr. and Mrs. Douglas Andrew Blake
have the honour of announcing
the marriage of their daughter
Sharon Anne
to
Mr. Jeffrey Paul Fowler, Jr.
Date (spelled out—no numerals)
Year (spelled out—no numerals)
Location

Please note that the year is included on an announcement although not on an invitation.

Check the following points, and make your decisions:

1. Stationers will show you small response cards and envelopes to enclose with the invitations, but only you can decide whether or not to use them. Many people consider such cards to be more suited to business or charity affairs than wedding invitations. Even while agreeing in principle, some hosts reluctantly decide to use them to assure prompt responses, especially for sit-down affairs.

2. An address for responses is needed—unless you include response cards. A return address on the envelope is *not sufficient*.

3. If the church is one of many in a large city, include its address.

4. Some invitations will be mailed out of town, so be sure to include the city or town where the festivities will take place.

5. On the reception card, state "Reception and dinner" if that is your plan.

6. Another decision before you can order your invitations: Should you choose engraving or thermography? Thermography imitates engraving handsomely. Engraving used to be recognizable by lightly rubbing a finger over the lettering and feeling the unevenness. Thermography, however, also has raised letters at a fraction of the cost. To distinguish between the two, one must look at the reverse side to see the indentations made by the engraving plate. A fine distinction.

Do not consider ordering printed invitations—not even for a moment!

At last! You are ready to order the invitations. Count the cards in your file (or ask your computer to count for you), and jog your memory by reading the next section of this chapter. Then order *more*. The largest portion of the cost is engraving the plate or setting up for thermography. The cost of an extra twenty-five or fifty invitations is minimal. Also order extra envelopes to allow for mistakes. At the same time, order your announcements if you plan to send them.

For a small wedding of fifty or fewer, you or your mother may hand-write the invitations, or use your own, a friend's, or a professional's talent for calligraphy. Use plain, finest-quality, fold-over paper in ivory or white.

You may follow the conventional, formal wording and spacing or write a carefully worded, friendly note.

Double-check Your Guest List

1. Have you made an equitable division of guests between the groom's family and yours? (See p. 12.)

2. Although the groom's parents are well aware of the wedding date, be sure to mail them an invitation. They will want to keep it.

3. Have you invited parents, brothers, sisters of the members of your wedding party?

4. Count on sending a separate invitation to any person eighteen years or older. Exception: You may send joint invitations to two or more brothers or sisters living at the same address.

5. Close friends living at a great distance consider it a compliment to receive an invitation. However, if you feel that an invitation seems to call for a gift, you may prefer to send announcements to less intimate friends. This is your decision.

6. If you wish single guests to bring a date or escort, write on the inner envelope beneath the name, "Please bring an escort (or date)," or you may enclose a note. You might prefer to ask for the name and address and mail a separate invitation—especially to a friend's fiancé. This is where those extra invitations will come in handy.

RULES FOR ADDRESSING

For a change of pace let's play a game. Can you find nine mistakes in the following address?

> Mr. & Mrs. Chas. D. Blake and Family
> 33 E. 25th Ave.
> San Francisco, CA 94112

You probably spotted them all. If you did not, here are the rules for addressing:

1. Write *and*. Symbols are not permissible.

2. *Charles,* not *Chas.*; write the name in full. No abbreviations except *Mr., Mrs., Ms., Dr.,* and *Jr.*

3. *David,* not "*D.*" No initials are permissible. If you do not know what the initial stands for, omit it.

4. Never *and Family.*

5. Write out *East* and *West, North* and *South.*

6. Write out *Twenty-fifth.* Use no figures except for the house numbers and zip code.

7. Write out *Avenue.* Also *Boulevard, Road, Lane, Street,* and so on.

8. Spell out *California.* Again, no abbreviations.

9. All invitations must be addressed by hand, preferably in permanent black ink. Never, never typewrite an address.

ADDRESSING INSTRUCTIONS

Use your file cards, and address carefully. Check each card as you finish. Follow this guide:

A. To a husband and wife:
   Outer envelope: Mr. and Mrs. Joseph Guest
   Inner envelope: Mr. and Mrs. Guest

B. To a husband, wife, and children under eighteen:
   Outer envelope: Mr. and Mrs. Joseph Guest
   Inner envelope: Mr. and Mrs. Guest
                    Elizabeth and John

C. To a married couple when the wife retains her maiden name:
   Outer envelope: Mr. Kenneth Guest and Miss (or Ms.) Barbara Townsend—written on one line
   Inner envelope: Miss (or Ms.) Townsend and Mr. Guest

D. To a widow, or if separated:
   Outer envelope: Mrs. Robert Guest (never Mrs. Alice Guest)
   Inner Envelope: Mrs. Guest

E. To a divorcée who has not taken back her maiden name:
   Outer envelope: Mrs. Barbara Guest or Mrs. Barbara Townsend Guest
   Inner envelope: Mrs. Guest

OR

Outer envelope: Mrs. Townsend Guest
Inner envelope: Mrs. Guest

The latter example—using one's maiden surname combined with the former husband's last name—was always the established, traditional, and *only* "correct" way. This custom is gradually becoming outdated through usage. If you know your friends' preferences, carry on their way; otherwise, take your choice.

F. To a single woman:
Outer envelope: Miss Carolyn Guest (or Ms.)
Inner envelope: Miss Guest (or Ms.)

This rule applies to girls of any age—no matter how young.

G. To a single man:
Outer envelope: Mr. Thomas Guest
Inner envelope: Mr. Guest

The title "Mr." is not used until high school age. Until a boy is eight he may be addressed as "Master."

H. To two sisters:
Outer envelope: The Misses (or Misses) Elizabeth
                    and Mary Guest
Inner envelope: The Misses (or Misses) Guest

I. To two brothers:
Outer envelope: The Messrs. (or Messrs.) John and
                    William Guest
Inner envelope: The Messrs. (or Messrs.) Guest

J. To two persons living at the same address, same
   or different sex. If one of each, the lady's name
   is on the first line:
   Outer envelope: Miss (or Ms.) or Mr. First Last
                   Miss (or Ms.) or Mr. First Last—
                   on separate lines
   Inner envelope: Miss (or Ms.) or Mr. Last Name
                   Miss (or Ms.) or Mr. Last Name—
                   on separate lines

GENERAL ADDRESSING INSTRUCTIONS

1. Place invitations in the inner, ungummed envelope. Folded invitations are inserted with the folded edge
down. Envelope-size invitations are inserted with the
engraved side facing the flap of the envelope.
   Enclosure cards are inserted as follows:
      —With envelope-size invitations, stack the
        enclosure cards in this order: Place the recep-
        tion card on top of the invitation. The re-
        sponse card (if you are using it) will come
        next, engraved side face up and tucked under
        the flap of its own little envelope. Insert all as
        a unit in the manner explained above, facing
        the envelope flap.
      —With four-fold invitations, slip the cards in-
        side in the same order, and all facing the flap.

2. With improved printing techniques, ink no
longer smudges, and protective tissues are not needed.

3. The inner envelope is inserted into the outer
envelope upper side up, so the writing faces the
unaddressed side of the outer envelope.

4. If friends help you address, see to it that the same person addresses both the outer and inner envelopes. If return addresses are written by hand, they should also be written by the *same* hand.

5. Remember: use black fountain pen ink—no ballpoint or felt tip.

6. Professional addressers are available. Some specialize in calligraphy. They can be located through your stationer, a bridal shop, or the classified section of your telephone book. Specify that they follow your instructions for addressing.

7. Always mail invitations and announcements sealed, first class mail—never metered.

8. As you know, it is improper to write "and Family" on the outer or inner envelope. Equally improper is "No Children." Is there a way to keep mothers from bringing uninvited children to the reception? Yes. Telephone to suggest that they may bring their children *to the ceremony*. Explain that you must limit the number of reception guests. They will understand.

9. Announcements are addressed in the same manner as invitations.

10. Announcements should be mailed *after* the wedding takes place—the same or the next day.

11. No announcements should be sent to those who received invitations.

12. When addressing, sealing, and stamping are completed, sort the envelopes by destination—local, out of town, and foreign. Mailing foreign letters by surface costs a few cents less than by air but is only worth the saving if time is not a consideration.

13. Invitations should be delivered from four to six weeks before the wedding.

Divorced Parents

Divorced parents have been advised over and over again to resolve or forget their differences and to conceal any antagonistic feelings. They will be admired if they consider the bride's feelings on her important day and handle their roles with dignity, cooperation, and apparent ease.

What is seldom mentioned, however, is the bride's responsibility to help ease a difficult situation. If she is mature enough to marry, she is surely mature enough to be sensitive to her divorced parents' feelings. If her parents are friendly, she will have no problem. If they are not, she should be realistic and accept the fact that she cannot act out a fairy-tale version that does not exist.

For example, if her father should refuse to give the bride away unless the "other woman" attends, and if she knows this would be unbearable for her mother with whom she lives, then let her ask a brother, godfather, grandfather, uncle, or friend to do the honors.

Although situations vary widely, fortunately there are solutions or compromises for every problem. If financing the wedding should become your sole responsibility, simplify it into an affordable plan.

INVITATIONS

An experienced stationer will have suggestions and samples for you to consider. Your own desire for harmony will guide you.

1. The parent who is closer to the bride, or the one with whom she lives, usually issues the invitations. Grandparents, a brother or sister, or other relative may take over the honors if circumstances demand.

2. If the mother of the bride has remarried, she may send the invitations as "Mrs. New Husband's Name requests . . ." or, "Mr. and Mrs. New Husband's Name request . . . at the marriage of *her* daughter . . ." (giving the daughter's *full* name).

If the remarriage is of long standing and the bride is closer to her stepfather than to her natural father, she might ask him to give her away.

3. Sometimes an envelope contains both the mother's invitation to the wedding and the father's invitation to the reception, along with the desired response address. He may give his daughter away at the altar. If he has remarried, his wife's name may appear with his on the reception invitation as host and hostess.

4. If the parents are separated but not legally divorced, they should ignore their differences and issue invitations under the normal procedure.

5. If the mother has not remarried and issues the invitations, she uses her divorced name. Reread item E on page 86, and decide whether or not to stay with tradition.

THE REHEARSAL DINNER

The rehearsal dinner presents another possible snag. It is customary for both parents to attend. Again, if they are friendly there is no problem. Talk over difficult situations in advance to find the least awkward solution. Perhaps carefully arranged place cards will satisfy, although in extremely sensitive cases, one or the other parent may decline the dinner invitation.

SEATING IN CHURCH

1. The mother of the bride sits in the first pew on the left. If she has not remarried, she may sit alone, or invite a relative to join her—but not a casual escort. If she has remarried, her new husband will have been escorted to her pew earlier, and she may walk out with him after the recessional. As an alternative, the head usher or her usher-son may return to escort her; her new husband will follow immediately behind.

2. After giving the bride away, her father sits in the second or third pew on the left with his parents or his wife if she attends.

3. If the groom's parents are divorced, the same seating arrangements apply to them, but on the right-hand side of the aisle.

RECEIVING LINE SUGGESTIONS

1. If the bride's mother gives the reception, she stands in the line. The bride's father attends as a guest and does not stand in the receiving line.

If she has remarried, her husband does not stand in line; he acts as host.

2. Suggestions if the bride's father gives the reception:

—Remarried or not, he may relinquish his place in the line to the bride's mother—a happy solution.

—If he has not remarried, the bride's mother may stand in the line either next to him or separated by the groom's parents.

—If he has remarried, he may stand first in the line. His wife does not stand in the line; she acts as hostess. The bride's mother is a guest.

Your Personal Trousseau

The word "trousseau" might sound old-fashioned or archaic, like "dowry." Dictionaries, however, offer no synonym. Trousseau is defined as a bride's outfit of clothes and linens. So *whatever* clothes and linens—old or new—you bring to your marriage, become a part of your trousseau. In usage today, buying a trousseau means replenishing and augmenting.

Parents love to help replenish and augment to whatever degree they can afford, and to share their daughter's thrill of acquiring her "trousseau."

Selecting is a highly individual and personal matter, but a few suggestions follow:

1. What a joy to start your married life with an assortment of pretty, new, feminine, and romantic lingerie.

2. It used to be considered essential to send a bride off with enough clothing to last at least a year, until her young husband could provide for her. Today's bride prefers the option of adding when the seasons, styles, and needs change. Some generous parents allow their daughter a "credit" for an additional outfit or two during the year.

3. Some marriages will bring about a change of residence, location, or manner of living, so buy accordingly.

4. Look over the clothes already in your closet to decide what can be renovated to fit your future life-style.

Make a list of what is required to fill out your wardrobe.

CHECK THESE	ON HAND	NEEDED
Slips		
Bras		
Panties		
Hose		
Nightgowns		
Robes		
Hostess outfits		
Shoes		
Suits		
Dresses for daytime		
Dresses for evening		
Coats		
Gloves		
Handbags		
Hats		
Accessories		
Sweaters		
Sport clothes		

Your Linen Trousseau

This is the ideal time, and your opportunity, to review and evaluate your family's style and customs from your growing-up days. Decide which practices you admire, are comfortable with, and want to maintain, and which styles and standards of your own you want to establish.

Linens will probably come to you as shower or weddings gifts. If you live away from home, you already have some of the basics. Maybe your parents have shared, or will share, some of their expendables with you. From all these sources you have a good start.

The following section is simply a worksheet. Add or subtract to suit yourself.

For monogramming, see page 101.

CHECK LIST OF LINENS

Dining room

When dining table woods are beautiful, the bare-table look is attractive, but deceiving. One still needs small mats or doilies under the china.

> Breakfast sets. Handsome plastic mats are cheerful and practical.
> Luncheon mats or cloths, and napkins.
> Informal dinner.
> Formal dinner.

Table cover for buffet suppers, and lots of extra
napkins.
Tip: When you serve curry or other foods that
stain, use white napkins. They can be bleached
instead of ruined.
Cocktail napkins (frequently received as gifts).
Bridge table sets.
Tray cloths.
Doilies.

Bedroom

Top sheets (three for each bed).
Fitted bottom sheets (three for each bed).
Pillow cases (four for each pillow).
Blankets, comforters, or electric blankets.
Blanket covers.
Duvets and covers.
Mattress covers.
Bedspread and dust ruffle, when you know your
décor.

Bathroom

Bath towels.
Hand towels.
Washcloths.
Bath mats.
Guest towels.

Kitchen

Dish towels.
Dishcloths.
Cleaning cloths.
Dust cloths.

Stationery

This list of basics will help you choose the letter papers that suit *your* life-style.

1. Everyday paper for household or business-type letters—even chatty letters to long-time friends. Convenient if printed with your married name, address, and phone number on single sheets.

2. Engraved fold-over informals or single French cards are useful for invitations, responses, short thank-yous, and to enclose with gifts. "Mr. and Mrs." and "Mrs." only, are made from the same die. They can take the place of engraved calling cards in most instances. If your address is relatively permanent, it may also be engraved on this stationery.

3. A box of perfectly plain, best-quality white or off-white paper, for formal responses and letters of condolence.

4. Good quality note paper or correspondence cards for notes and invitations. Monogram if you wish, or postpone ordering a die. As time goes on, both your needs and taste could change. In the meantime, handsome bordered papers in interesting color combinations are available.

5. Printed memos or postcards are handy for brief information or to use as enclosures.

6. If you use your maiden name professionally, order business stationery to fit your needs.

7. You will find more information about the use of initials and names in the next two chapters.

Initials and Monograms

1. Towels and bed linens: The first initial of your husband's surname is the largest or accentuated initial of the monogram, usually centered, and flanked by the first initial of your first name on the left, and the initial of your maiden name on the right.

2. Stationery: Monogram is the same as for linens. However, if you retain your maiden name, stationery may be engraved or processed with both your names— yours on the first line, his on the second.

For engraved calling cards and informals, use *Mr. and Mrs.* and full name including the middle name. *No initials.*

3. Silver: Use the single initial of your husband's surname, or follow the style for linens and stationery. Silver may be engraved on the front or back of the handle tips.

Silver is often passed down from one generation to another. If it is already monogrammed with initials other than your own, use it with pride.

4. For fun and informality, such as on bar glasses, you can combine your and your husband's first-name initials.

Signing Your New Name

1. If you take your husband's name, you will sign your name on checks and legal papers as given name, maiden name, husband's name: Barbara Townsend Long.

2. In letters to close friends, you will always be Barbara.

3. To those who will recognize your new name, you will sign Barbara Long. If they might need a clue, sign Barbara Townsend Long.

4. For committee-type or household business letters, sign as in item 1 on this page. Under your signature write in parentheses (Mrs. Kenneth Long).

5. Some couples agree to hyphenate their surnames such as Mr. and Mrs. Kenneth Townsend-Long. Infrequently, they reverse their last names. In this example it would be Mr. and Mrs. Kenneth Long-Townsend.

6. If you do not assume your husband's name, clarify by using a printed letterhead with your name alone and, for joint letters, your name on one line and his on the line below.

7. Did you know that you may legally use two or more names? You may, therefore, keep properties and selected accounts in your present name, while using your married name socially and for joint assets.

If a time occurs when you are uncertain about which name to sign, you may sign both names this way: One name / a.k.a. / other name. (The initials a.k.a. stand for "also known as.")

8. Do not sign letters jointly as Kenneth and Barbara, except for gift and greeting cards. Instead, mention your husband in the body of the letter.

Your Gifts: Selecting, Registering, Displaying

What joy and excitement to select your very own china, crystal, silver, furniture, and accessories. Here is your chance to create your first home in the taste and style you want.

Even if you know your life-style will be modest at first, try to project your thinking to envision a later time in your lives when you will entertain with more than stainless steel and wooden salad bowls. If you have to store those more elegant possessions in the family's attic for a while, it will be a double treat when you finally retrieve and use them.

SELECTING

Silver

Silver is so expensive that you would be thrilled to acquire one piece at a time. In deference to your friends, ask the store personnel to quote the cost of individual pieces, not complete place settings.

Plan to enjoy your sterling flatware daily instead of saving it for company. It will last for generations. With use, silver attains a beautiful mellow look.

Crystal

No matter how costly it is, it chips and breaks. Ask any long-married person about her crystal inventory. She will probably report something like, "seven goblets, nine wineglasses, a dozen sherbets" (because the sherbets are used less often).

Aim for sixteen or eighteen instead of the usual dozen of each kind, and don't burden yourselves with the most expensive crystal in the world.

China

If you choose an expensive make of china, as with your silverware, again ask the store to quote prices of individual pieces instead of place settings.

You might not even want complete matching place settings. Many people of style believe their dinner tables are more interesting if they use a different pattern for each course as long as the feeling is compatible—not delicate china and bold pottery at the same meal.

Everyday Dishes

Register your everyday dishes too. Being less costly than your good china, the price range will please some donors. Try to select a pattern you won't tire of with constant use.

Gourmet Homewares

Gourmet specialty shops stock excitingly handsome and utilitarian homewares. Brides love to register their needs and desires at such a shop. Besides cookware, you will be tempted to register everything else you see. If you register in such a shop, be sure to tell friends who ask.

REGISTERING

1. If you make a point of registering your desires in a wide price range, it will indicate that you would be

as delighted to receive an inexpensive bud vase or pepper mill as you would a sterling silver platter.

2. Register your gifts in more than one store. If you live in the suburbs but are inviting friends from the city to your wedding, register in both places.

3. Keep a list of the stores where you have registered for those thoughtful friends who inquire, "Where are you listed?"

4. If you register the same patterns or duplicate objects in more than one store, update the listings periodically. Notify the other stores when the desired quantity has been reached.

5. If no one will be at home to receive gifts when they are delivered, make special arrangements with the stores to deliver only on certain days or to hold the gifts until you notify them.

DISPLAYING

Part of the guests' fun at a home reception is viewing the gifts.

If the reception is held away from home, one does not take gifts to display; however, there will be other opportunities to show them off. Invite relatives, a few interested friends, and your bridesmaids to drop in at teatime or in the morning for a cup of coffee.

To display your gifts, use card tables placed side by side, folding tables, or improvise by using sawhorses with boards or plywood on top. Cover the table with a white cloth—satin if you wish. Ribbon bows or sprays of artificial white flowers are very pretty. You might even have your florist do a professional display table, if you are in an extravagant mood.

Gift-display tips:

1. Do not exhibit cards of donors.

2. Do not display checks. An empty envelope or a card bearing the word "check" may be placed on the table, if you wish. This is optional.

3. Arrange the gifts as artistically as possible. Keep in mind the donors' feelings by the thoughtful placement of each gift. For example, a little ceramic salt and pepper shaker would look attractive next to your everyday pottery but would show to disadvantage near a Steuben bowl or a silver tea set.

4. Separate similar gifts.

5. If you receive exact duplicates, display only one, unless the identical gifts make a handsome pair. In that case, display them both.

6. Try to borrow plate and tray display racks from a gift shop.

7. When displaying dinnerware, crystal, and silver, use only one place setting.

8. You may exchange duplicate and unusable gifts *after* the wedding, but not at the risk of hurt feelings. With the exceptions already noted, all gifts should be displayed.

You need not—in fact, *should not*—tell donors about the exchanges. Thank them for the gift they sent, not the substitute.

9. Appoint someone to be in charge of gifts that guests occasionally bring to the reception. How much better if the donors had sent the gifts in advance! It is not considerate of the other guests to open packages during the reception—even at a home wedding.

ANOTHER VIEWPOINT

Much is said throughout this book about gifts—registering, receiving, exchanging, displaying, and writing thank-you letters. There are circumstances, however, when the bride and groom sincerely do not want any gifts at all. Maybe they are about to consolidate two households into one, or they have other reasons.

Since the words "No gifts please" are specifically forbidden on wedding invitations, what can you do? You can tell close friends how you feel and rely on them to spread the word. If despite your wishes some friends send gifts, do not make an issue of it. Just accept graciously.

Houseguests

Even after you considered the hazards and alternatives, mentioned on page 21, item 61, did your hospitable nature overrule your practical sense of caution?

Here is one more idea before you succumb: If you just can't bear the thought of housing out-of-towners elsewhere, consider a compromise. Your parents might invite them to stay for a few days of happy reminiscing *after* the wedding.

Getting ready for houseguests, whether before or after the wedding, will mean preparations and perhaps some reorganizing, but the anticipation of seeing relatives or close friends keeps it all from becoming a chore.

No two homes have identical facilities or are run the same, but everyone can consider the following suggestions and reminders. They should help make your preparations easier and your houseguests more comfortable.

1. Remember jet lag.

Flying from the West to the East Coast presents little problem the first day. However, don't schedule a dinner party for westbound travelers the first evening unless they arrive early enough to take a rest. By the dinner hour, their built-in clocks will scream "bedtime."

Transoceanic flights create even more severe time lags.

2. Invite for a specified length of time. Planning will be easier if you know exactly how long guests will stay.

3. Give houseguests both privacy and freedom to do what they want—rest, read, walk, or sit in the sun.
Don't schedule every moment; however, it is your town, and you know what it has to offer. Make suggestions and give them a city guide marked with the "don't miss" sights.

4. Before retiring, settle plans for morning—breakfast together or each on his own (with a kitchen-orientation tour).
No coffee-holic should have to wait. Set up the coffeepot at night, and let the first one up plug it in.

5. If you are used to running your home informally, everyone will be more comfortable if you don't strain to suddenly change your style.

6. In preparation, spend a night in the guests' quarters, or give the rooms an extremely critical eye. Check:
   —Reading and makeup lights.
   —Assorted short reading matter.
   —Pen, pencil, note paper.
   —Check bedding carefully to see if there are enough blankets and if they need cleaning or rebinding.
   —Extra pillows for reading in bed.
   —Clothes hangers, including the special kind for skirts and trousers.

—Supply the bathroom carefully. In addition to the essentials, think about the conveniences guests might like: scissors, cleansing tissues, bath oil, lotions, hair spray, nail file.
—Will they need ashtrays?

7. Make the guest room more beautiful with a bouquet of flowers or a plant, and more comfortable with a pitcher or vacuum jug of drinking water.

8. Feel free to keep your own important appointments or to do household errands. Your guests will understand.

9. If your guests have other friends who live in the area, assure them they are free to make engagements on their own.

10. Unless you run a hotel-style establishment, let guests make their own beds.

11. If hired help assists in the house, guests will probably follow the custom of leaving a tip. I would prefer to pay a bonus and mention to my guests that the matter has been taken care of. Some guests still like to send a personal gift to longtime regular help.

12. When I have houseguests, I begrudge every moment I spend in the kitchen. One shopping bout and a few hours of concentrated cooking can take care of several days' meals with the aid of your freezer. You might inquire beforehand about possible special diets, so you can buy accordingly.

13. Spell out in detail for both the men and women what type of clothes they will need for the weather and the activities you have planned.

14. If your guests are unfamiliar with your area, give them transportation assistance on the wedding day. Options: Ask friends to pick them up; lend them your car; engage a driver; if they have their own car, give them the same help you gave the drivers, namely a map, time to leave, estimated travel time, and plenty of leeway in case they aren't expert "pathfinders."

Now here is your surprise reward in return for your hospitality. Nothing could be more priceless in the last few days before the wedding than an extra pair of hands, legs, ears, eyes, and one sane brain. Count on one of your houseguests to be a buffer to answer the phone and doorbells, accept deliveries, post gift numbers in the register, press out a wrinkle, and generally relieve and shield you by making minor decisions.

Special Pew Holders

I cannot sufficiently stress the importance of pew arrangements. Who wants fiery-tempered relatives on this special day?

1. The bride's family and friends sit on the left side of the church; the groom's family (as guests of honor) and their friends sit on the right.

2. Send reserved-pew cards to family members and those special friends you wish to honor. Ask the groom's parents for their list, and send reserved-pew cards to their special friends too.

Reserved pews are referred to as "within the ribbons," because those rows are often identified by extra flower or ribbon decorations.

3. Specially engraved cards for pew holders can be purchased from stationers, although more often the bride's mother writes the information on plain cards or her engraved calling cards.

4. It is better to send special pew cards *after* you receive acceptances. This way you avoid the possibility of having empty seats or the problem of rearranging the seating plan.

5. At a small or less formal wedding, you may dispense with sending pew cards. Just notify those honored guests by telephone. You must still inform the ushers by giving them a list of names and assigned pews.

Example

Pew 3 Brides Reserved Section
Mr. and Mrs. Special Guest

Mr. and Mrs. James Perry Standish

Please present this card to usher

SPECIAL PEW HOLDERS

Bride's (left) side:

Name _____ Pew _____

Name _____ Pew _____

Name _____ Pew _____

Name _____ Pew _____

Name _____ Pew _____

Name _____ Pew _____

Name _____ Pew _____

Name _____ Pew _____

Name _____ Pew _____

Name _____ Pew _____

Groom's (right) side:

Name _____ Pew _____

Name _____ Pew _____

Name _____ Pew _____

Name _____ Pew _____

Name _____ Pew _____

Name _____ Pew _____

Name _____ Pew _____

Name _____ Pew _____

Name _____ Pew _____

6. Review this list with the head usher. Be sure he understands all arrangements.

The Wedding Rehearsal

All the steps you've taken and the detailed plans you've made are finished! Now it's time for this happy and important rehearsal for the Main Event tomorrow. Afterward you will enjoy the rehearsal dinner for the bridal party, their wives, husbands, fiancés, both sets of parents, and perhaps a few out-of-town guests. A very special evening.

All members of the wedding party should be present at the church, along with the clergyman, organist, soloist (if any), and church wedding director. You will receive complete directions about everything—the processional, ceremony, and recessional.

NOTE: I have deliberately omitted descriptions of specific denominations. You need be concerned only with your own, and you will have discussed details of rituals in earlier conferences with your clergyman.

Almost all of today's brides ignore the old superstition that required the maid or matron of honor to stand in for them. How much better to feel poised and at ease with the mechanics and ready to experience the ceremony to its fullest. This is the time to carry one of the mock bridal bouquets, fashioned of ribbons at a shower.

There are a few decisions to make, based on the advice of the wedding director's experience:

1. If you have both a maid and matron of honor, you must decide which one will hold your bouquet during the ceremony. You must also decide who will hold the groom's ring if you are having a double ring ceremony.

2. Decide whether you wish your honor attendant or the groom—your *husband* by then—to fold back your veil at the altar.

3. You may have a preference as to the step your bridesmaids will use in the processional. The "hesitation step" is not as popular as it once was because it is difficult to keep perfect balance. The more natural, slow walk in time to the music is easier and more graceful.

4. If there is to be a soloist, decide at what point she should sing. Suggestion: Before the wedding march at a short cermony or during the ceremony at a nuptial mass. Ask the wedding director for her opinion.

5. *Processional:* The groom, best man, and minister will enter the church from a side door and stand near the altar, looking toward the bride.

The ushers walk down the main aisle in pairs. They are followed by the bridesmaids, usually walking singly and graded by height to avoid sharp contrasts. Next is the maid or matron of honor. If both are in attendance, the one chosen to hold the bride's bouquet at the altar enters immediately before the bride and her father. Exception: A junior bridesmaid would follow the honor attendant, then a ring bearer, and finally the flower girl. These three are optional.

An unusual, but pretty, variation: I once saw the bridesmaids walk in single file up the two side aisles from the front to the rear of the church. They then followed the ushers down the center aisle.

6. *Recessional:* The maid of honor, paired with the best man, will follow the bride and groom. If there are the same number of bridesmaids as ushers, they follow in pairs. If their numbers are unequal, the bridesmaids may walk first, followed by the ushers, or an extra usher may be placed amid the others.

The flower girl or ring bearer may follow the bride and groom. If they have performed well, some parents decide not to tempt fate further and take them in hand at that point.

7. Which arm? Take whichever arm you wish, but decide at the rehearsal. If you take your father's right arm, he can reach his pew more easily, especially if your train is long. Also, this will put you nearer the groom's side of the church walking down the aisle and closer to your own friends and family in the recessional, when you will be on your groom's right arm.

8. Now is the time, while you are at the church, to make sure the ushers understand about the reserved pews.

9. If this is the ushers' first experience, remind them to ask each guest, "Friends of the bride or groom?" Friends of the bride are seated on the left; friends of the groom on the right. However, if one family is represented by fewer guests, ask the ushers to seat the guests indiscriminately for the sake of balance.

10. Instruct the ushers that just before the ceremony is to begin, grandparents should be escorted to their pews. Next, the head usher will escort the groom's mother to the first pew on the right. If her son is an usher, he may do the honors. Her husband will follow a step or two behind.

11. Procedure: The mother of the bride is the last person to be seated, escorted by the head usher, or her son, if he is an usher. No one may be seated after her. Late arrivals will have to stand in the entry until after the members of the wedding party reach the front of the aisle.

After a few seconds' pause in the music, it will change to the wedding march or other chosen selection. This change will herald the precise moment the processional is about to begin. The bride's mother will then stand, and make a quarter turn, in time to see the first attendant start down the aisle.

Guests will follow her lead, standing and turning toward the aisle to view the procession of attendants followed by the bride on the arm of her father.

The Reception

If your plans do not call for a reception, or if some guests have been invited to the ceremony only, the receiving line quickly forms in the vestibule of the church. The wedding party and the mothers take the same positions as shown below, without the fathers.

If everyone is invited to the reception, the bridal couple should be driven without delay so the festivities can start promptly.

A wedding reception, like any other form of entertaining, should be planned with your guests' enjoyment in mind. Don't leave details and timing to chance and assume that all will work out well. Plan meticulously, then enjoy!

RECEIVING LINE POSITIONS AND PROCEDURES

1. Mother of the bride
2. Father of the bride (optional)
3. Mother of the groom
4. Father of the groom (optional)
5. Bride
6. Groom
7. Matron of honor
8. Maid of honor
9. Bridesmaids

1. Ushers and the best man do not stand in the receiving line.

2. It is customary for the bridesmaids to take their positions in the line—and a pretty picture they make, indeed! Less traditionally, either for lack of space or in the interest of time, only the maid of honor stands with the wedding party.

3. If the bride has no mother, her father, another relative, or a close friend may stand at the head of the line.

4. Frequently the fathers greet and introduce their friends from a position ahead of the line and not too near it.

5. Ask the photographer to take the receiving line pictures quickly. *Very* quickly.

6. Set up a table for the guest book well ahead of the receiving line, staffed by a special friend. Do not attempt to have a roving guest book attendant. No matter how hard she tries, she is certain to overlook a few guests.

7. Instead of letting guests stand interminably waiting in the hot sun or cold wind to go through the receiving line, cheer them with glasses of champagne. Also arrange that someone—perhaps the acting hostess or a friend—encourages them to mingle with other guests, then reenter the line when it thins out.

Have a table placed where they may leave their used glasses before they go through the receiving line.

8. At a home reception, arrange to divert some of the guests to the gift display before they go through the line (see p. 106).

9. When guests reach the receiving line, they expect to say only a few words of admiration and good wishes. Greet each person cordially. Let him know you are happy he is there, then promptly and graciously introduce him to the next in line. Encourage your bridesmaids to do the same. By taking only a few moments, you will be doing *all* your guests a favor.

10. An announcer is sometimes used, but only for a very formal wedding. He asks the name of each guest, then relays it quietly to the mother of the bride or to whoever is standing first in line. Your catering service can provide you with an announcer, or if you wish, an usher can substitute for a professional. Usually, however, one can depend upon considerate guests to help you by quickly giving their names. It also helps to review the acceptance list frequently ahead of time.

11. Because no one will be free to circulate among the guests until receiving-line duties are finished, alert close friends or relatives to watch out for specific out-of-town friends who might be standing apart. For this alone a professional hostess can be a help and comfort.

12. At a club, hotel, or restaurant reception, the host should pay gratuities in advance to the cloakroom, rest room, and parking attendants. At a large home reception, arrange for help in parking, either by engaging a parking service or qualified sons of neighbors or friends.

TYPES OF MENUS

Your menu depends upon the time of day. If you are trying to minimize expenses, select the time that requires the least amount of food and service.

Timing is important. If the ceremony is scheduled for *early* afternoon, do not expect guests to stay for a supper or dinner. Serve a suitable afternoon menu instead.

The Wedding Breakfast

The "breakfast" is, in fact, lunch. It takes place after a morning or noon ceremony and may be served at tables—usually three courses—or from a buffet with a number of selections.

Drinks may be served before lunch, in addition to wine with lunch and champagne at cake-cutting time.

Afternoon Reception

A tea or cocktail menu, with the addition of a wedding cake, is appropriate. Make it as simple or as elaborate as you want—from punch, pretty homemade open-faced sandwiches, and wedding cake, to a catered repast of hot and cold canapés, choice of drinks, a buffet of substantial, elegant selections, and wedding cake. Even on the tightest budget, it costs nothing to make everything appetizingly attractive. You can rent or borrow plates, but do not settle for paper ones.

Without a doubt, an afternoon wedding when no one expects substantial food can be the least expensive.

A fine and perfect wedding can be produced "on a shoestring" when friends help. In place of hired waiters or waitresses, preteen and early teenage daughters of friends pass the platters of goodies. The youngsters, dressed in their best outfits, feel honored, and so do the guests. Some friends will contribute flowers; others will provide dainty sandwiches. Yes, it can be done beautifully though economically if need be. When friends band together to make the day special for you, their warmth does indeed make your unforgettable day even more exceptional.

Dinner

A *late* afternoon reception may be prolonged until a dinner or supper is served, either at tables or from a buffet. A six or seven o'clock ceremony will definitely include dinner.

A dinner requires arranging the seating with place cards, and providing seating charts with names in large print, or individual cards with names and table numbers (see p. 24, item 77).

This detailed task is time-consuming and not much fun, but worth making each guest feel specially considered.

At a large dinner you might find it preferable to place congenial friends together, while at the smaller rehearsal dinner you intentionally intermingle your guests.

Evening Reception

This is similar to the afternoon reception. Frequently a late supper is served, especially if guests stay for dancing.

THE BRIDE'S TABLE

Even if the guests serve themselves from a buffet, it is acceptable to have a bride's table at a large, formal wedding. This table is for the wedding party—without parents, escorts, or dates but with husbands and wives, if possible.

A long, narrow table is arranged with everyone seated on one side facing the room. Use place cards. The bride and groom are seated in the center—the bride on the groom's right, the best man to her right, the maid of honor to the groom's left.

The table is decorated with white flowers. The cake may be placed in front of the bride and groom as long as it does not conceal them from their guests, or on a separate table.

If all the guests are to be seated, parents may have a special table. Traditionally the groom's parents are guests of honor, the mother seated to the right of the bride's father, the groom's father to the right of the bride's mother. Grandparents, the clergyman and his wife, and closest friends are seated at the parents' table.

DANCING

When the bride and groom are ready for their first dance, the orchestra swings into their favorite dance tune (see p. 77 for the order of the dances). Although the bride and groom will be the first to dance, they need not be first in line when a buffet is served.

TOASTING THE BRIDE

Ask the musicians to play a fanfare so friends will gather around for the toasts and cake-cutting procedure.

Just before the cake is cut, the best man toasts the bride. Other toasts may then be offered by the groom and both fathers. The bride and groom drink to one another and to their parents. After the toasts the best man will read a few congratulatory telegrams or mailgrams.

CUTTING THE CAKE

The bride uses a knife decorated with ribbons or flowers. Perhaps she received an engraved one as a wedding present or wishes to use a family heirloom. With the groom's hand placed on hers, the bride cuts the first slice from the lowest tier of the cake, and as a symbol of sharing their lives, she gives her husband the first bite; he gives her the next. This is a lovely custom when handled gracefully and unselfconsciously. It is not amusing to see a beautiful bride or handsome groom smeared with gooey frosting.

The cake is then cut by a waiter or waitress and served to the guests. The top tier may be removed and saved to wrap, freeze, and enjoy at your first anniversary celebration.

Individual boxes, each containing a slice of cake, are seldom seen today. The significance of this charming favor was to place it under one's pillow and dream of one's future spouse; those already married would be granted a wish.

THROWING THE BOUQUET

Before leaving to change into going-away clothes, the bride—with the groom at her side—tosses the bouquet to her bridesmaids. Toss it from a stairway, an upstairs window, a balcony, or any attractive raised setting. If none are available, improvise with a small platform covered in white. Sometimes other unmarried women gather to catch the significant next-to-be-married symbol. Do your best to keep very young girls away so the eligible young women can have a fair chance at the bouquet. Brides also throw a bridal garter to the bachelors as their next-to-be-married symbol.

CHANGING TO GOING-AWAY CLOTHES

The maid of honor accompanies the bride to help her change. Bridesmaids may follow. Ushers accompany the groom. Just before the bride and groom are ready to leave, the maid of honor notifies the parents of the bride and groom so they can have a brief, private good-bye.

LEAVING THE RECEPTION

While you are changing, little ribbon-tied packets of rice, confetti, rose petals, or bird seed will be passed to the guests. (Some of the very young would love that assignment.) Remember that rice can sting faces and make stairs dangerously slippery, and rose petals stain rugs. Paper rose petals are available at wedding supply shops and are the best choice; confetti rates second best. The ecology-minded opt for bird seed—out of doors, of course.

Before you make a choice and go to the trouble of making or ordering the packets, check with the reception locale management. Hotels and clubs seldom permit the use of rice, and sometimes forbid all of them. You have freedom of choice only if your reception is at home.

The best man will drive the getaway car or see that the one he ordered is ready. The final dash for the car—

another *don't miss* photograph—is a happy and memorable moment for you and your guests. Away you go!

Four Variations of Planning

1. If you plan to be married out of town or at a family-only affair, the reception may be held at a later date. Either set of parents or the bridal couple themselves may give it.

This delayed reception is usually more informal and follows either a tea or a cocktail party plan (see p. 34).

2. If you plan to hold the reception in a church community room, find out exactly what equipment is provided: coffee makers, refrigeration, china, glasses? Important: Inquire about possible restrictions as to alcoholic beverages.

3. Reception halls are available, especially in or near large cities. Many are equipped to provide everything—a complete package. "Everything" can include rooms in which to dress, flowers, photographers, refreshment, even someone to officiate at the ceremony if desired.

Such halls have a variety of banquet rooms to accommodate any number of people, and they offer anything from a simple tea menu to an elaborate dinner.

As with all services, you will find a wide range of price and quality.

4. For the bride on her own or at a very small wedding—whether at a friend's or your own apartment, home, or garden—there is no recessional. When the

ceremony ends, you and your husband turn and stand in place to receive good wishes and congratulations.

If parents are present they tend to take the same positions as in church—the bride's parents on the left, the groom's parents on the right.

Select appropriate refreshments for the time of day, and serve them with ease—perhaps from a buffet table that features your wedding cake.

With attention to flowers and other details, small can be beautiful.

For the Groom

You have fewer details than the bride to take care of, however, you have definite responsibilities. Here is your special check list:

1. Arrange for a conference with the clergyman; both you and the bride should be present. Other prenuptial meetings might be required.

2. Beat the deadline for turning in your and your family's guest list. You will endear yourself to your future mother-in-law.

3. Purchase a wedding ring for the bride.

4. Grooms often give their brides-to-be a personal gift such as a piece of jewelry.

5. Purchase a permanent keepsake for each of the ushers. Your gift to the best man may be a similar article but a bit more expensive. Typical gifts are cuff links, leather box, pewter mug, picture frame, silver jigger, a fine desk or dresser accessory, key chain, travel gadget. These gifts may be given at the bachelor dinner or the rehearsal party.

6. Arrange your business affairs:

—Draw a will.

—Change the beneficiary on your life insurance.

—Arrange for a joint bank account and perhaps a separate account for your bride.

7. Make arrangements for the honeymoon. Traditionally you pay for the honeymoon unless generous parents provide the gift.

Send a deposit, and be sure you have on hand a letter of confirmation. If you are planning to stay in a nearby hotel and will arrive late, register in advance so you may go directly to your room, or ask your best man to help with these arrangements.

8. Make financial arrangements for home or apartment and utilities.

9. Get a physical checkup. Get a dental checkup. Get your blood test if your state requires one.

10. Discuss with your bride what you and the men in your wedding party will wear. She will set the pattern for the wedding by deciding on the setting, time of day, and degree of formality of her wedding gown—all of which establish the type of attire the men should wear. Cooperate graciously.

Don't let a rental establishment persuade you to wear inappropriate suits, such as dinner jackets before six in the evening or colorful outfits at any time (see p. 134).

As soon as you and your bride select the style, reserve the number of outfits you will need. Notify local ushers to go immediately to have their measurements taken. If your groomsmen live out of town, the rental establishment will give you measurement cards which the men can have filled out by tailors in their places of residence. Beg your ushers to return the completed cards *promptly*.

The outfits will be reserved for you with preliminary alterations. Last-minute fittings, and adjustments if needed, can be made when the men arrive for the wedding.

11. Buy wedding ties for the ushers and best man, and gloves if they are to be worn. These are your gifts to them.

12. Go with your bride to get the marriage license.

13. Making the reservations for out-of-town men in the wedding party is your responsibility, as well as paying for the accommodations. Lucky you if local relatives or friends offer to house the groomsmen.

14. Arrange to be billed by the florist who is making the wedding bouquets. You are expected to pay for the bride's bouquet, corsages for the mothers, and boutonnieres for yourself and the ushers. Going-away corsages—once considered a "must"—are out of fashion as of this writing, but styles come and go, and then come again. If corsage wearing should ever become popular again, you will add that to your florist bill.

All these flowers will be selected by the bride. You *may*, if you wish, pay for the bridesmaids' bouquets, although they are usually considered part of the décor.

15. You pay the clergyman's fee—actually an honorarium, which he either keeps or donates to the church. The amount is left to your discretion; just remember

that the more elaborate the wedding, the larger your contribution should be.

Place new currency in an envelope and give it to the best man. He will hand it to the clergyman in the vestry room, either before the ceremony or immediately after when the marriage certificate will be signed.

16. Do not put off your haircut until just before the wedding. Avoid that new-shorn look.

17. The bachelor dinner is usually arranged by the best man. It may be hosted by you or your ushers. Try to schedule it early in the week before the wedding.

18. Blacken the soles of your shoes. They will look better if you kneel at the altar.

19. Be of good cheer.

Men's Attire

As the preceding chapter, "For the Groom," stated, the type of men's attire will be established by the pattern of the wedding—its setting, time of day, degree of formality, the bride's gown, and season of the year.

Customs vary in different parts of the country for no discernible reason, so this book can only state what is generally considered proper.

1. *Formal Daytime:* Oxford gray cutaway coat, striped gray or black trousers, lighter gray waistcoat. A starched wing collar with an ascot, or a starched regular collar with a four-in-hand tie. Gray doeskin gloves (remove gloves at the reception). Plain-toed black shoes and black socks. Pearl or black studs, pearl or gold cuff links.

2. *Semiformal Daytime:* Short Oxford gray director's coat, double-breasted gray waistcoat, four-in-hand tie. Gray doeskin gloves (remove at reception). Plain black shoes and black socks. Pearl or gold jewelry.

3. *Informal Daytime:* Oxford gray or dark blue suit, white shirt, four-in-hand tie, black shoes and socks. Black or gold jewelry.

Summer Informal in the country or suburbs: Navy blue blazer with gray or white flannel trousers, or a lightweight summer suit.

4. *Formal Evening:* Tail coat, white piqué waist-coat, stiff-bosomed shirt with starched wing collar and white bow tie. Black dress pumps and black socks. White kid gloves. Pearl jewelry.

5. *Semiformal Evening*—not before six o'clock: Black or midnight blue dinner jacket, black or midnight blue vest or cummerbund and matching bow tie. White dress shirt. Black plain-toed shoes or dress pumps. Black socks. Black or gold jewelry.

Summer Semiformal: The same as above, except you may wear a white dinner jacket, if that is an acceptable style in your locale.

6. *Informal Evening:* Dark business suit. Plain white shirt. Black shoes and socks.

GENERAL INFORMATION

—The groom, best man, ushers, and both fathers wear the same type of suit. If the fathers rebel, they do not stand in the receiving line.
—All the ushers' ascots or ties should be alike, but they should be different from the groom's and best man's.
—All the ushers should wear the same variety of boutonnieres, such as white carnations, while the groom and best man wear lily-of-the-valley boutonnieres pinned to their left lapels.
—A tuxedo before six o'clock in the evening? Never!
—*Plain* white shirts are best.

Best Man's Duties

You are an extra pair of legs and an extra head for the groom. Your responsibilities are many, varied, and important. Do whatever you can to cooperate with and relieve the groom.

1. If suits for the groom and men of the wedding party are rented, it is your responsibility to pick them up and to return them after the wedding. Check the pockets for personal belongings. Each man will pay for his own outfit.

2. The groom will give ties and gloves. You could assist him by determining the men's glove sizes and purchasing them.

3. Sometimes the groomsmen host the bachelor dinner. You can help organize both the dinner and finances. Other times the groom gives this party. If so, you can make the reservations for him, help select the menu and drinks, and see that the ushers know the time and place.

4. The ushers and best man customarily purchase a gift for the groom. As best man, you organize this effort.

5. Help the groom with honeymoon reservations if necessary.

6. If the bridal couple plan to stay in a nearby hotel after the wedding, they can be preregistered, then go directly to their room. You can register for them and bring the key to the groom. Swear on your honor not to divulge their plans.

7. Although there will be a head usher, you are in charge of all the ushers. Remind them *where* to be and *when,* for the parties, rehearsal, the church, the reception.

8. The bride and groom might wish to hide the honeymoon car, in which case you can place their luggage in it ahead of time. When they leave the reception, you drive them to their car, unless you have arranged for a taxi or limousine.

9. On the wedding day, you will help the groom dress. Don't wait until that day to check out his clothes and accessories—and your own as well. Put everything in one place—studs, shirt, tie. This is especially important if you are dressing elsewhere.

Take the wedding ring to the church in a safe pocket or on your little finger, if it will fit.

10. Make sure the groom has the wedding license, which must be signed by the clergyman and witnesses— probably you and the maid of honor. Take it to the church yourself.

11. You pay the clergyman. The groom will give you an envelope with the fee inside. Pay the clergyman quietly in the vestry, either before the ceremony or after, while you witness the signing of the marriage certificate.

12. You give the first toast to the bride, usually just before the cake is cut.

13. You read a few congratulatory telegrams or mailgrams immediately after toasting the bride.

14. Dance with the bride, the mothers, and the bridesmaids. Yes, you are busy.

15. Occasionally a groom will ask his father to serve as best man. If so, a few of the best man's duties listed here can be taken over by the head usher.

What a help you are! What would the groom do without you?

Ushers' Duties

The ushers have been selected because they are the groom's close friends. In that capacity as honored and special friends, they add much geniality to prewedding and wedding reception festivities. For the wedding itself, their duties are specific.

1. Ushers pay for their own rented outfits. The groom will tell you where he has made arrangements for them. Go as soon as possible to have your measurements taken, and go later for your fitting when scheduled.

2. Ushers, as a group, give the groom a memento. One popular gift is a silver box engraved with your signatures. Your wedding gift to the bride may also be given by the entire group of ushers or individually.

3. In the festivities immediately preceding the wedding, if you are unmarried or unattached, you are expected to escort bridesmaids to parties—regardless of personal whim.

4. Attend the wedding rehearsal. On time.

5. On the wedding day arrive at the church an hour ahead of time.

6. Pin your boutonniere to your left lapel. Ignore the buttonhole; it is only decorative.

7. Offer your right arm to each woman guest and escort her to a pew. Ask if she is a friend of the bride or groom. Bride's friends sit on the left of the aisle; groom's on the right. As the church fills, it may be necessary to balance the number of guests on either side of the aisle. Simply ask if the guest would mind. When you escort a woman, the men and children in her group will follow you to the pew. The same procedure is followed with unaccompanied men, but you do not offer your arm.

8. The head usher seats the mother of the groom. Her husband follows a few steps behind. The head usher escorts the mother of the bride to her pew. She is the last person to be seated. If her son is an usher, he may escort his mother if she prefers. At a wedding I attended, the mother of the bride was escorted by *two* sons who were ushers. A meaningful variation.

9. At a very formal wedding, a white canvas runner furnished by the florist may be laid on the center aisle. If the runner is in place ahead of time, the ushers escort guests to their pews from the side aisles. At other times the runner is placed by two ushers after the mother of the bride is seated.

10. Familiarize yourself with the special pew-holders' seating plan.

11. If the church has a balcony, an extra usher may be assigned to seat guests there. Since late-arriving guests will probably be seated in the balcony, it is not necessary

for this extra usher to be in the processional although he should join the recessional.

12. Two or more ushers may be asked to return after the recessional to escort the bride's and groom's mothers and grandmothers out of the church. More often, the bride's mother and father lead the way, followed by the groom's parents; the guests follow, alternating left and right, row by row.

13. The ushers are responsible for transporting the bridesmaids from the church to the reception. Promptly.

14. As an usher, you might be asked to substitute for an announcer. If so, merely ask the guest's name and repeat it to the first person in the receiving line.

15. Mild practical jokes can be funny as long as they do not embarrass, endanger, or disrupt.

Bridesmaids' Duties

Bridesmaids have an important role. What could be more reassuring to the bride than knowing she is surrounded by her closest friends who will support her before, during, and after her wedding! Bridesmaids bring their gaiety, beauty, and the warmest of feelings to the wedding and reception.

Bridesmaids often plan a shower or other party for the bride; they have their gowns fitted on schedule; they join in the prenuptial party time. When The Important Day arrives, they walk down the aisle with happy and relaxed smiles.

MAID OF HONOR OR MATRON OF HONOR

You as the honored attendant have more responsibilities than the other bridesmaids:

1. Help the bride dress on her wedding day.

2. Hold her bouquet, and possibly her gloves, during the ceremony.

3. If it is a double ring ceremony, you hold the groom's ring.

4. If the bride wishes, you may fold back her veil at the altar.

5. You stand in the receiving line with the other attendants. You can help speed the progress of the line by introducing the next bridesmaid clearly and with pleasure.

6. After the receiving line dissolves, mingle with the guests and have fun.

7. Help the bride change from her wedding gown to her going-away outfit.

8. It is your duty to inform the parents of the bride and groom when the newlyweds are ready to leave.

9. As the best man is an extra pair of legs and an extra head for the groom, so are you for the bride on her exciting day. You can help smooth her way.

Flower Girl and Ring Bearer and Junior Bridesmaid

1. The ring bearer should wear his best dress-up suit—navy blue, or perhaps white linen in the summer.

2. He carries a white satin, brocade, or tapestry pillow with the wedding ring (the real one or a substitute) stitched on.

3. The flower girl's dress should harmonize with the bridesmaids' gowns, and her bouquet should be scaled down in size.

4. Instead of a bouquet, the flower girl may carry a basket of paper rose petals to strew along the bride's path.

5. If the wedding procession includes both a ring bearer and a flower girl, they precede the bride and her escort in that order. In the recessional they follow the bride and groom and walk side by side.

6. Parents of the children pay for their wedding party clothes.

7. Include the flower girl, the ring bearer, and their parents in your arrangements for transportation.

8. The children probably will be too young to join the receiving line.

9. Give each child a keepsake gift and a photograph of the wedding party. They will treasure it.

10. Invite their parents to substitute for them at the rehearsal dinner.

11. A junior bridesmaid—age ten to fourteen—has the same duties and privileges as other bridesmaids.
> —In the processional she follows the maid or matron of honor and precedes the ring bearer and flower girl, if any.
>
> In the recessional she walks immediately behind the bride and groom unless there is a flower girl or ring bearer, in which case she follows.
>
> —Her gown should be modified to suit her age.

The Groom's Parents

Because almost all wedding responsibilities and decisions traditionally belong to the bride and her parents, the groom's family may feel superfluous—even the groom feels forgotten at moments during the hectic rush of bridal activities. But did you ever hear of a groomless wedding? Never! He is indispensable, and so are you as his parents.

You will play an important role at the ceremony and reception as special guests of honor. Please read this entire book in order to understand and empathize with all the bride must do—then follow this chapter for your own list of do's and don'ts. You will feel at ease if you know exactly what is expected of you.

THE ENGAGEMENT

As soon as your son tells you "She said yes," telephone the bride-to-be to express your pleasure that she is going to be your new daughter. Next, telephone her parents and arrange to call on them or invite them to dinner. Talk about the bride. Your interest in her can contribute to your son's happiness. If her parents live out of town, phone immediately. Also write them an enthusiastic letter, and a separate one to the bride.

After the engagement has been announced, you might like to give a tea or cocktail party to introduce the bride to your friends. If not, you may entertain for her or for both of them after their wedding trip.

When you plan a party, remember that a shower hosted by a member of either family is taboo.

If you live nearby, you will be invited to showers for the bride. Take a gift. If you live out of town, you might receive courtesy shower invitations. If possible, send a shower gift in care of the hostess.

Your Financial Obligation

If this wedding is to follow tradition, the bride's family will pay for the entire wedding and key it to their own finances. In the past if the groom's parents were more affluent, they occasionally assisted by assuming, or contributing to, a portion of the expense, such as the bar, flowers, limousines. They sometimes offered to pay for wedding announcements they wanted but which the bride's parents did not need. This help was given behind the scenes, with a private understanding between both sets of parents.

These days, however, one may find both families openly sharing expenses—following the custom of some foreign countries. In that case the names of both sets of parents appear on the invitations:

Mr. and Mrs. Bride's Parents
Mr. and Mrs. Groom's Parents
request the honour of your presence
at the marriage of
Jennifer (plus last name)
to
Mr. Groom's full name . . . etc.

The groom's obligations are listed starting on page 130. If he is still a student, no doubt you will assist him.

Give the bridal couple a present. Suggestions: silver, a family heirloom, a more extensive honeymoon trip than the groom can afford, furniture for their new home, a check.

Give the bride a personal gift—perhaps a piece of jewelry.

In rare situations the groom's parents offer to give the wedding; for example, if the bride is an orphan with no other relatives to take over, or if her parents live in a foreign country or too distant city.

If you host the wedding, the invitations should be worded:

> Mr. and Mrs. Your Name
> request the honour of your presence
> at the marriage of
> Miss Bride's Name
> to their son
> Mr. Groom's Name . . . etc.

This is the correct form for a church wedding. A home wedding invitation would read "request the pleasure of your company."

Note this exception when "Miss" is correct, or Ms. if the bride prefers.

GENERAL PLANS

The remainder of this chapter is directed to the traditional wedding. *Cooperation is the keynote.* Cooperate with all the bride's plans but do not attempt to make any decisions of your own.

1. Limit your guest list to the number of places the bride's parents allot you. They may be restricted by space or budget limitations.

2. Submit your guest list on or ahead of schedule. This is important!

3. Spare the bride the tedious task of organizing your guest list. Make a separate file card with each guest's full name (no initials), address, and zip code. Follow the form shown on page 6 of this book. Use the same procedure for your announcement list, provided announcements are to be ordered. Ask the bride if she would like you to use cards of a different color.

4. Offer to help address invitations, but do not be offended if the bride and her mother find it less confusing to do it themselves.

5. Even though you might prefer another style or period of china, silver, or furniture, remember that the young couple must feel free to carry out their own tastes without outside pressure.

6. Occasionally, but not customarily, a groom invites his father to serve as best man. Don't feel disappointed if your son chooses a close friend. Cooperate with his decisions, too.

WHAT TO WEAR

The bride's mother will select her outfit first, then expect you—the mother of the groom—to coordinate your color and style with hers. Refer to page 16, item 38. If you are not enthusiastic, take heart. When your daughter marries, *you* will have first choice.

The groom's father should dress in the same style of suit as the men in the wedding party—provided their outfits are traditional.

REHEARSAL PARTY

The groom's parents frequently offer to give this party— usually a dinner preceding or following the rehearsal. This will be your greatest—perhaps your only—opportunity to contribute to an important prewedding affair. Besides, you will have fun.

1. *Where to hold the party*

Give the party wherever convenient—at home or in a club, hotel, or restaurant.

Even if your dinner will take place in a city where you are strangers, you can make advance arrangements. Check to see if your home club has reciprocal privileges with clubs in other cities. If not, consult the bride's parents for their recommendations, then arrange details by direct correspondence with the hotel or restaurant.

2. *What to check*

Ask the catering department to submit:

- —Several detailed menus from which to choose
- —Wine list
- —Complete prices, including predinner drinks

Specify:

      —Private dining room

      —Desired arrangement of tables such as T or U shape, or small tables

      —Table appointments like candles and linens

      —When you order flowers, agree on exactly what you want and the cost, because prices vary startlingly in different sections of the country. You need not confine the decorations to white—any timely, romantic, or colorful theme is appropriate.

A gracious gesture: give the floral arrangements to the bride's parents or grandparents to take home.

3. *Whom to invite*

Consult the bride for her list. In addition to the members of the wedding party, expect to include the attendants' husbands, wives, and fiancés and—if the bride wishes—those special relatives and friends who will travel some distance to the wedding.

The clergyman and his wife are invited only if they are close friends of either family.

4. *How to invite*

Even if you are certain everyone knows about the rehearsal party plans, send written invitations. This will avoid confusion about the time and place, and the possibility of overlooking a guest. An informal note will do, or write the information on your engraved cards.

5. *At the dinner away from home*

Arrive well ahead of time to arrange place cards, check the tables, and be ready to greet your guests.

Your party will be more successful if you arrange the seating to mingle age groups and local residents with out-of-towners. By writing names on *both* sides of the place cards, you can refresh the memories of those guests who have just met and who dislike admitting they've already forgotten each other's names.

For a large party post a seating chart near the entrance with names written or typed in *large* letters.

At the dinner at home

Perhaps you can set up enough card or folding tables to seat everyone. Again, use a seating chart.

Your plan might call for an informal buffet, with guests expected to take their plates and sit in groups "anyplace." Rather, show your thoughtfulness by posting a chart listing groups of six, eight, or ten, directing them "to the den," "on the porch," "living room around the fireplace,"—wherever you have a comfortable seating arrangement and a few conveniently placed tables.

6. *A toast to the bride*

The groom's father should be prepared to give a toast. He may mention his new family-to-be, but his main words should be directed to the bride.

7. *What about music and dancing?*

Make the party as simple or as elaborate as you wish. If you decide on music, plan it for only a short time. Rehearsal dinners usually break up early if they are held one or two nights before the wedding.

8. As a surprise you might engage a photographer or videographer, or ask a friend to record the rehearsal dinner party. These pictures will be a welcome addition to the wedding album.

9. *Paying the bill and tipping*

At your club (or one you are using), sign the chit in advance. A service charge will be added to your bill.

At a restaurant or hotel, to avoid being presented with the bill in front of guests, you may arrange to:

—Give the maître d'hôtel your credit card when you arrive, then sign away from the table.

—Arrange a charge account ahead of time, and have the bill mailed.

—Quietly excuse yourself and take care of the bill while guests are drinking coffee.

Tipping can also be handled discreetly:

—Hotel catering departments do not expect tips; arranging is their business.

—One does not tip a restaurant owner.

—At your request, a hotel or restaurant will add an agreed-upon percentage to your bill to take care of gratuities, and distribute them equitably. This procedure eliminates the need for hasty mental arithmetic calculations.

—Don't forget the wine steward, the captain, and the waiters.

—If a person patronizes the same restaurant regularly, he probably gives the maître d' a Christmas present. If this is a one-time visit, a tip will be expected.

—For that added thoughtful touch, tip the cloakroom and parking attendants in advance. Make it clear that the attendants are not to accept additional tips from the guests, but to inform them that the matter has already been taken care of.

IN CHURCH

And now for the proud moment!

Shortly before the processional starts the grand-parents will be seated. Then the head usher will escort you, the groom's mother, to the first pew on the right-hand side. Your husband will follow a step or two behind and take the aisle seat. If you have another son in the wedding party, other than the best man, ask that he accompany you.

The bride's mother is always the last person to be seated.

If your relatives attend the wedding, be certain that pews are reserved for them and that they identify themselves to the ushers. Refer to page 113 for important procedures.

Leave the church immediately after the recessional. The receiving line cannot start until you have taken your place in it.

RECEIVING LINE

Now the solemnities are over and it is almost time to relax. Your last official duty is to stand in the receiving line and do your part to keep it moving smoothly. Don't hold up the line by chatting at length with your own friends but introduce them promptly to the next person in line. When the line disbands you will be free to visit.

Sometimes the fathers stand in the receiving line. This decision is made by the bride. Refer to page 93.

Mothers sometimes keep their gloves on, but if the bride's mother removes hers, follow her lead. Gloves will not be worn at a home wedding.

When it is time for the bride and groom to leave on their honeymoon, one of their attendants will take you to them for a quick hug and a kiss.

And then—give a silent toast to their enduring future happiness.

After the Wedding

Even when the beautiful wedding is over and the bride and groom have left, you—the mother of the bride—will still have a few things to do.

1. Entertaining out-of-town guests: Following an afternoon wedding, perhaps you will have a supper for them, along with members of the wedding party and relatives. If the wedding is in the evening, you can arrange a brunch or lunch for the following day.

2. If the top layer of the wedding cake was fruitcake, wrap it well and store it in your freezer for the bride and groom's anniversary.

3. Mail the announcements of the marriage the day after the wedding, unless a friend has been charged with this responsibility.

4. Answer telegrams sent to you. Keep those sent to the bridal couple for them to acknowledge later.

5. Have the wedding gown professionally "heirloomed." Use a cleaner who specializes in preservation. He will carefully dry-clean and remove spots, enfold it in a special kind of paper that does not react chemically with the fabric, and preserve the gown in an airtight container to prevent yellowing.

6. If you send handwritten acknowledgment cards to those whose gifts arrived late, the gesture will be appreciated. For example:

"Your gift arrived after Jason and Lisa left on their wedding trip. Lisa will write to you personally when they return."

7. Take a few days for self-pampering renewal. You might want to let the telephone or doorbell go unanswered, or perhaps you prefer to hear your friends' compliments. After that, go on a weekend jaunt with your husband.

What a wonderful feeling of satisfaction to know that *nothing was left undone* to help your daughter create that perfect wedding. Whether your part in the preparations was a large or small one (maybe she only wanted your emotional support), whether the wedding was an extravagant catered affair for hundreds of guests or a small gathering where home-baked cake was served, it was an equally joyous occasion.

You know that your part was done with love and for love. What more is there!

Here Comes the Bride— Again

or

Always a Bride, Never a Bridesmaid!

ANNOUNCING YOUR ENGAGEMENT

You can hardly wait to share your joy with the world. But pause a moment! If you or your fiancé have children, they should be told first, along with both sets of parents. If you are a widow, tell your parents-in-law before they hear the news from outsiders. If you are divorced, be certain to tell your former spouse, and also your former in-laws if you have kept in touch with them. Next, tell your close friends, and the news is guaranteed to travel with rocket speed.

Provided neither of you is waiting for a divorce to become final, you might announce your engagement at a dinner, tea, or cocktail party, or simply at a family dinner (see p. 29).

Please disregard the information on page 30 about formal newspaper engagement announcements, because it applies to first marriages only. An item about your wedding plans might appear, however, in a news column, which differs from a formal engagement announcement. After the marriage takes place, many newspapers will print the wedding announcement.

You may certainly wear an engagement ring when both divorces are final.

YOUR GENERAL PLAN

How remarkable that no two weddings are ever identical, nor should they be! Each is unique! The guidelines are here to give you help, reminders, alternatives, a smattering of advice—but only a minimum of rules. Select the items that have meaning for *you*. You might or might not want to incorporate the symbolic traditions mentioned on page 24, item 78.

Circumstances vary too much to advocate a single pattern for all second weddings. If you analyze your particular situation, your wedding plans will begin to fall into place. Consider your category: Are you a young widow? A young divorcée? A mature widow? A mature divorcée? Was your marriage annulled? Is this your second marriage but your fiancé's first? Is he much older than you? Younger? Have you children? Has he? Young or grown? Has your former spouse remarried? Are relations amicable? Are finances a consideration? Is it your first marriage but your fiancé's second? Answer: Plan any style wedding that pleases you both. While you and your former husband were separated, he died. Are you a widow or divorcée? Answer: A widow. Are you about to remarry your former husband? Suggestion: Quietly is best.

You see how thinking about *your* specific situation has helped you focus on what is best for *you*. The differences between the wedding of a young widow and that of a mature widow are quite apparent. If you are very young, you might want your father to give you away once again at a fairly sizable gathering. The mature widow would probably feel more comfortable inviting only families, children, and close friends.

You have much to think about:

—Strive for a completely different atmosphere from your previous wedding: different location, music, decorations, cake, dress, everything.

—You might prefer an intimate ceremony, followed by a large reception the same day or at a later date.

—If you eloped or arranged a nontraditional wedding the first time, you may yearn to savor the experience of a glorious, traditional ceremony. If so, you will find beautiful bridal gowns—maybe with a dramatic bright sash, and in a more sophisticated style than you would have chosen as a younger bride.

—Some couples delight in surprising friends. You could take off to a faraway place to marry, and celebrate with a party after you return home. Instead of sending formal wedding announcements, why not notify friends by postcard from your wedding locale?

—Another surprise suggestion: Invite friends to a party—not a reception. When guests arrive, they will find to their surprise that they are celebrating your marriage which took place earlier that day.

—Have you always heard that one should wait at least a year to marry if either is widowed? A younger couple is more inclined to wait, while some older couples might decide, based on their experiences, that life is already too short. In either case, postpone announcing your engagement until close to the wedding date.

WHO WILL OFFICIATE?

Throughout this book I have used the word "clergyman" to cover officials of all denominations, whether they be priest, rabbi, minister, pastor, or other. One can also be married by a judge, governor, chaplain, registrar, justice of the peace, or ship's captain, to name a few.

Before forming even a tentative plan, make an appointment, along with your fiancé, to meet with your clergyman. In preparation for your visit, please study pages 40 to 43 in detail. Although most of the items apply to church weddings, much information serves equally well for second weddings, and in locations other than churches. Check the items you wish to consider.

If you find that the clergyman is restrained by church tenets from officiating at a marriage of divorced persons, or those of different religions, he might still be able to refer you to someone who will gladly perform the ceremony. Others will bless a marriage in a meaningful rite after it has taken place.

Some churches restrict the location of the ceremony to the clergyman's study, or to a side chapel, while others permit the use of the main altar. If your guest list is small and the church is huge, you might inquire about seating your guests in the choir stalls. You probably will not need to reserve the church for a rehearsal for this simplified plan.

A SMALL WEDDING

If your previous wedding was large and lavish, this time you might decide to limit the guests to family members and close friends—perhaps no more than fifty. The ceremony could take place in a church, club, hotel, or in your own or a friend's home, apartment, or garden.

Small does not mean dull or somber. Small, in this event, means intimate, personal, joyous, warm, and *very special*.

The Bride's Dress

Select an outfit appropriate for the season and time of day, in a becoming color or off-white. You will look glorious!

> —No formal wedding gown or wedding veil.
> —A pretty silk or wool suit for a morning wedding.
> —A street-length dress or outfit for an afternoon wedding.
> —Long or short "cocktail dress" for an evening candlelight ceremony.
> —No gloves or hat at a home wedding.
> —Flowers to compliment your outfit.

Attendants

Instead of thinking "maid or matron of honor, or bridesmaid," think "attendant-witness." At a small wedding, that is what both you and your fiancé need. You might ask a sister, your best friend, or the friend who introduced you to your husband-to-be, or as suggested later in this chapter, your child could do the honors. Perhaps your attendant's wardrobe already includes an appropriate dress in the same degree of dressiness as yours, and in a compatible color.

Rehearsal and Rehearsal Dinner

At your initial meeting with the clergyman, perhaps he saw no need for a rehearsal. Even so, you need not forgo a festive dinner one or two evenings before the wedding. This is an ideal time for you and your fiancé to gather together your families and out-of-town guests. A thoughtful relative or friend might volunteer to host the affair. Otherwise, you and your fiancé can give the party yourselves.

Even if the party is small, ask someone to take photographs for you to add to your wedding album.

Receiving Line After the Ceremony

At a small wedding there is seldom a processional or recessional. You and your husband will turn and stand in place after the ceremony. Your guests will come forward to greet you.

Flowers

Flowers always add warmth and beauty to the decor. To avoid a possible disappointment, choose a florist whose work you have seen and admired—one whose suggestions are compatible with your taste.

Photographs

Be sure to record this day of days. Either ask a friend to take the pictures or engage a photographer (see p. 67).

What to Serve at Your Small Wedding

Your menu can be as festive and special as you wish. You will find suggested types of menus for different times of day on pages 123 and 124. Let your imagination and talents soar to new heights!

Music

Music always adds to the enjoyment. Suggestions: violin, guitar, zither, accordion, piano, or an organ rented for the day. At home, if you want to keep it

simple, why not enjoy your favorite tapes? You can set
them up in advance.

A Large Reception

As suggested earlier, you may wish to have a large reception either immediately following an intimate ceremony or at a later date. When making your plans,
consider this not as a repeat performance but a completely new one. Call upon your ingenuity.

Starting on page 36, you will find a detailed de-
scription of cocktail parties—one plan you might wish
to follow.

Starting on page 120, the chapter entitled "The Reception" describes in detail a more formal event. Check
the items that suit your plan. You would probably decide
to dispense with the bride's table, and to reduce the
receiving line.

Wedding Cake

Here is your opportunity to be creative—with the
help of a master pastry cook to carry out your original
ideas. Your cake may be artistically decorated with fresh
or icing flowers in your favorite colors, or you may
substitute an entirely different dessert. Decorated petit
fours, éclairs, or flamed crepes suzettes are possible
choices.

Dancing

You and your husband will want the first dance
together, but if you wish, you may disregard the rest of
the traditional routine.

Catering

If you make reservations for your reception in a club, hotel, or restaurant, its catering service will take care of you. If you plan to hold it elsewhere, check "Caterer," page 60, to select the items that apply to your plan.

Photographers

See page 67. Select from all those reminders to assure that nothing has been forgotten.

INVITATIONS AND ANNOUNCEMENTS

Your choice of invitations will depend upon the size of your wedding. Please refer to the chapter starting on page 80 for a general guide. It outlines the conventional formulas for small, informal weddings and for larger weddings and receptions.

Decisions must have been easier in the "olden days" when rigid rules of etiquette forbade formal weddings for second-time brides. Even well into the nineties, the majority of brides marrying again still prefer a smaller wedding followed by a larger reception. Maybe in the twenty-first century and another revision of this book, new customs will be born. For your particular use, you already have a number of options.

Invitations

—For a small wedding, handwritten or telephoned invitations are customary. Calligraphy is another attractive option.

—For a wedding reception, invitations may be engraved or thermographed, as described on page 83.

Parents may issue the invitations for a young second-time bride, using the standard format for a church wedding:

Mr. and Mrs. Bride's Parents
request the honour of your presence
at the marriage of their daughter
[given name/maiden name/married name (if retained)]
Barbara Townsend Long
to
Mr. Jeffrey Paul Fowler
(no initial)
etc.

For a wedding not in a church, or for the wedding reception:

Mr. and Mrs. Bride's Parents
request the pleasure of your company
at the wedding reception of their daughter
etc.

If the bride and groom issue their own invitations, the formal style for a young bride's church wedding is as follows:

The honour of your presence
is requested at the marriage of
[given name/maiden name/married name]
Barbara Townsend Long
to
Jeffrey Paul Fowler
etc.

For a wedding not in a church, or for the wedding reception:

> The pleasure of your company
> is requested at the marriage of
> etc.

An older widow usually uses her full married name, such as Mrs. Kenneth Lindsay, and the groom's full name is prefaced by "Mr."

The older divorcée uses one of two forms, as explained on page 86, item E. Invitations include the date, but not the year.

Announcements

- —Parents may make the formal announcement of a young bride's second wedding, using the formula "Have the honour of announcing . . ."
- —The bride and groom may make their own announcement, by following the same name formulas given above for invitations.
- —Announcements include *both* the date and the *year,* whereas invitations do not use the year.
- —Christmas or other holiday cards can carry the message of a recent marriage.
- —Personal notes to friends at a distance are the most appreciated. Friends want to hear everything about Mr. Wonderful.
- —Newspaper announcements can spread the news. Fill out and send the wedding forms or compose your own message to your local paper, and to others where you or your fiancé have connections. For more information, see page 30.

YOUR CHILDREN AND HIS

This is such a happy time for you and your husband-to-be; you want it to be happy for your and his children as well. Your relationship with them depends upon many variables such as the children's ages, another parent in the case of divorce, and individual personalities and situations. Because of those differences, it is impossible to set rules of procedure to cover every person or situation.

Your wedding can be a unifying, family affair if you both include the children in your plans as much as possible—a prelude to your future happiness. Here are a few ideas directed toward this goal:

1. Some couples, with the clergyman's approval, write vows which include the children in the ceremony.

2. If you have a child mature enough to understand and accept your marriage, perhaps he or she can stand with you during the ceremony. Occasionally a grown son will walk with his mother, and "give her away."

3. Even very young children can participate by carrying out small tasks. They can show guests where to hang their coats, or attend to the guestbook, or even pass small trays of canapés.

4. Children might want to join the dancers at the reception. If they are in their early teens and weren't exposed to dancing school, give them the opportunity to learn a few basic dance steps from your era. You could provide a dance teacher briefly at the rehearsal dinner, or sign them up for a short series of lessons at a dance studio, if they would enjoy it.

You remember the fairy tale about Cinderella and the "wicked stepmother." Comic strips and joke books love to play up that same stepmother situation. You and the children will surely recognize those stories for what they are—fairy tales and fiction. Discard them forever, and relish every moment with your expanded family.

BUSINESS MATTERS

Today's bridal couples frequently pay for their own weddings—not only those marrying for a second time, but also first-timers who are already independent.

A quiet, frank discussion about finances should take place before you say, "I do." Sit down together with pencil and paper, and calmly delve into your personal and business matters in detail—"mine, yours, and ours." If you both work or have separate incomes, consider each of the numbered items below.

It is important, however, before you can take final action on certain of the subjects, to decide what name or names you will use. Several options are discussed on pages 102 and 103. Please pay special attention to Item 7 on page 103, which explains the legal use of two or more names.

1. Decide which of you will be responsible for paying specific bills, such as household, clothing, entertainment, children's education, travel, insurance.

2. Have you each made out a new will or trust?

3. Will your bank accounts be separate, joint, or both?

4. Check the names and addresses on insurance policies, stocks, properties, and other legal papers.

5. Decide if you wish to keep your credit cards and store charge accounts in your name only, or in both names. Most women who have already established a good credit rating prefer to keep it intact and separate.

6. You might each have reason to discuss financial matters with your attorney, accountant, or your family, especially if children are a consideration.

Premarital agreements are frequently in order for second marriages, or for established brides and grooms. Sometimes this is a touchy, hurtful subject, whether requested by the groom or the bride. Neither one should sign an agreement until each has consulted his or her own attorney. Joint advice from a single source is inadvisable. Once reconciled to the satisfaction of both of you, put the matter out of sight and out of mind.

GIFTS

Are you concerned that friends might feel obligated to send gifts when they receive your wedding announcement? Don't worry; even an announcement for a first wedding does *not* call for a gift. Wedding guests will undoubtedly send gifts; other friends might or might not.

If you are in the midst of weeding out, and trying to coordinate two households into one, you might sincerely *not* want anything more added to your already crowded household. It would be so simple and convenient to include the words "No gifts," but etiquette frowns on using that expression on wedding invitations, while permitting them on invitations to anniversary and birthday parties. The only solution is to tell a few close friends, and ask them to "pass the word along." Obviously, you will not register gift selections.

If, despite your caution, some friends send gifts, just accept them graciously.

Some brides, however, might be delighted to receive presents. Following is a list of suggestions for the "over-supplied." If you like some of these ideas, you can place this book in a conspicuous place, conveniently opened to this page.

Gifts for the Bride Who Has Everything

Anything with bride's new initials or monogram:
> Initialed place cards
> Monogrammed playing cards and bridge scores
> Bridge table covers
> Address embosser
> Initialed or name-and-address letter paper
> Name-imprinted invitations forms
> Initialed bar glasses
> Towels
> Bed linen
> Table linen

Instead of Silver

> Decorative bowl
> Small art object
> Brocade or leather scrapbook
> Picture frame
> Table easel for picture
> Small table clock
> Gourmet basket

Everlasting address book with separate tabs for
   each name (convenient for coordinating the
   bride's and groom's lists)
Equipment for a favorite sport
Addition to a hobby or collection
Health club membership
Magazine subscription which highlights the cou-
   ple's interests
Wine or liqueur
Small radio

For a New Home

Gold house key
House plant
Garden shrub or tree
Garden furniture or accessory
Barbecue or hibachi
Extra telephone

If the Bride's Household and Tastes Are Known

State-of-the-art electronic appliances or gadgets
Replacement of everyday dishes and glassware

Nongifts to Honor the Couple

Donation to a charity in the couple's names
A group community service workday for children
   or the elderly (install needed playground equipment in a school, or plant a garden for a park
   or convalescent hospital)

A relative who might like to give a check could send a gift certificate instead.

All brides are cautioned time and time again to write prompt, enthusiastic thank-you notes. The second-time bride should show *twice as much* appreciation, knowing the gift came from the heart.

Showers are less often a part of the second-time wedding. If your same set of friends attended showers before your first marriage, they might say, or at least think, "Enough is enough."

A second-time bride was recently given this dreadful, unsolicited advice: "If nobody offers to give you a shower, give one for yourself." Fortunately, the bride knew that not even a relative should give a shower for her. But nothing should stop friends from entertaining at just-for-fun parties. They are the best kind!

CHECK LIST FOR A NEW START

Setting Aside Old Memories

Whether you are moving to a new home or staying in your own, plunge into a thorough, ruthless housecleaning—or rather, house clearing. It will take days to go through your papers, and every drawer and closet, so start this project immediately.

1. Out of consideration for your new husband-to-be, remove your former husband's pictures from prominent locations. You could hang them in the children's room.

2. Pack, label, and store old photograph albums.

3. Remove from sight, or discard, mementos such as sentimental birthday and anniversary cards, and love letters you might have saved.

4. Decisions, decisions! What to do with your beautiful, heirloomed wedding gown? If you are a widow with children, you might want to keep it for a daughter to wear. If you are divorced, you might prefer to pass it on to someone else who would appreciate it. You might find a bridal rental or resale shop who would buy it.

5. Your engagement and wedding rings: You can save them for a daughter or daughter-in-law, reset the stones in another piece of jewelry, or dispose of the set.

6. Check your linens. Were you clever enough to choose a man with the same initials? If not, the hems on good monogrammed sheets and pillow cases can be replaced with eyelet lace, or embroidered or patterned fabric. Sort through everything and decide which to keep.

7. Your desk will reveal dispensable items, such as calling cards, informals, and monogrammed letter paper.

8. If initials are engraved on your silver, definitely continue to use it. Silver is often passed down from one generation to another, regardless of the initials.

9. This is a good time to clear your wardrobe of unwearables, to bring up to date what you can wear, and to list items you need to round out your trousseau. Add a smart blouse or sweater to a good skirt; buy new

pants to go with that handsome silk shirt. Voilà! Two new outfits from one skirt and one shirt! You will remember to shop for lovely new lingerie, of course.

Consider this house clearing not as a chore, but as a joyful preparation for your newfound happiness.

The Nontraditional Wedding

During the seventies a number of brides preferred to plan unconventional weddings, independent of tradition.

In the eighties the trend reversed, and by the nineties tradition was reestablished, stronger than ever. Brides once again want a church wedding dressed in a gown "just like Mother wore." A few practices from the nontraditional era remain however, such as writing one's own vows (if permitted by the clergyman), and adding more personal and individual touches.

Most of this book is directed to those conventional, established customs; however, this chapter has been written to help the brides who have a sincere desire to carry out their own original and personal ideas in a beautiful way.

Because you want your wedding to express your own ideas, all the more reason to make it perfect.

Even the most informal-appearing affair cannot happen by itself. For any style of festivity or ceremony, you must decide exactly what you want, then carry it out step by step, carefully, completely, and consistently.

These three words say it all—care, consistency, and completeness.

As the opening chapter says, not every item will apply to every wedding. But many of the preceding details and reminders need to be considered whether the wedding is to take place in a church or a barn, a garden or a hilltop, at the shore of the sea or under the sea.

So read all that has gone before and use whatever applies to your plans; then note the few extra and special reminders for unconventional situations.

SELECTING A LOCATION

If your special dream setting is a mountain peak, a forest, a meadow, a sea or lake shore—any isolated out-of-doors location—you need to think of these things:

1. A reasonably accessible site.

2. Adequate off-the-road parking.

3. An alternate roofed location nearby in case of rain. A barn? A hall? A cabin? And a few umbrellas in the trunk of the car.

4. Privacy. A location least likely to be interrupted by the sounds of picnickers or hikers during the ceremony. Could you be lucky enough to know the owner of private waterfront or wooded property who might let you use it for the occasion?

5. If you choose a public park, check to see if you can and should reserve it.

6. A caution: Sounds do not carry well out of doors. Plan to speak distinctly during the ceremony.

WHO WILL OFFICIATE?

Keep in mind that you and your husband-to-be will
marry each other, and that a minister, rabbi, priest,
judge, or other official will simply *officiate* at your
marriage.

You will find that individual clergymen, even within
the same denomination, often vary in their attitudes
toward self-written vows and other changes in ritual.
Because of these varying attitudes you need to consult
with the officiator of your choice early.

1. Discuss with utmost frankness your desires,
plans, and innovations.

2. Find out if he will agree to any extra demands
upon him. (Need he fly in a plane . . . mount a
horse . . . sail in a boat?)

3. Tell him how much additional time he will need
to perform the ceremony away from his church.

4. If you wish two clergymen, each of a different
faith, to officiate jointly, consult with each one to complete the necessary arrangements.

5. Will you need to provide a kneeling cushion? A
raised platform as a focal point?

HOW TO INVITE

When you shop for invitations, you will find an almost
limitless and overwhelming number of choices of color,
size, design, and wording. This variety gives you the

opportunity to express your individuality or carry out a theme. Calligraphy is often used effectively for the invitations and addressing.

Some additions:

1. Include explicit directions and a map if you have chosen a hard-to-find location.

2. If you choose an outdoor location, specify where to meet in case of rain.

3. For the nontraditional wedding, perhaps the bride's and groom's parents will issue a joint invitation.

TRANSPORTATION

The bride's responsibility to arrange transportation for the bridal party to and from the wedding site becomes even more urgent if the location is hard to find. Include the groom's parents in your arrangements, especially if they are from out of town.

NOTE: Furnish each driver with a map or explicit directions—with a notation of the estimated time needed to reach the destination.

WHAT TO WEAR

What is the picture you wish to create? Is it Pastoral? Medieval? Victorian? Casual? If you dress to complete that picture, all will be perfect.

—Rich, bright tones are a throwback to the Middle Ages, when brides wore brightly colored

gowns trimmed with braid or jewels for their
summer outdoor weddings.

—A satin cathedral train among the thistles?
Inconsistent, wouldn't you say?

—Headdress. Whatever harmonizes with your
dress and the setting. You may choose no head
covering at all. A few ideas:

1. If out of doors, a short, fluffy, soft veil is
   pretty.

2. A picture hat.

3. Harmonizing "costume" headdress.

4. Flowers or leaves—using varieties that will
   not wilt quickly.

5. Ribbons entwined in your hair.

No matter which, your hairdo should be consistent with your outfit, not a showpiece in
itself.

—Bare feet? Yes, if they add to the total look.
No, if it might appear that you forgot your
shoes.

—If you will be far from "civilization," add first-
aid items to your emergency kit.

—Talk over with your husband-to-be what he
and the other men will wear—and agree on
the overall consistent look you want to present. As you know, dinner jackets are never
acceptable in the daytime.

FLOWERS AND DECORATIONS

Continue with your own ideas about the look of your wedding—the total effect. A few thoughts:

1. Preferable to hothouse blooms for an outdoor wedding are:
    —Varieties of garden flowers.
    —Baskets of field flowers if you can use them before they wilt.
    —A single flower.
    —Sheaves of golden wheat. They can add a rich note. Be forewarned that in Elizabethan times they signified fertility!

2. In a natural setting you will usually need little or no decoration except for the buffet table.

3. If you need to transport flowers some distance, be sure to select long-lasting varieties.
    —To prolong their lives, harden them as follows: Submerge the stems in a container of water and cut them under water to prevent air pockets from forming. Soak for several hours or overnight.
    —Transport them in tip-proof containers filled with cold water.

WHAT TO SERVE AT YOUR RECEPTION

Although this subject has been fully check-listed in the preceding pages, a few additional ideas for special cases follow.

1. Unless the site of the ceremony is also ideal for your reception, plan to serve refreshments elsewhere—your home, a friend's home, rented or public quarters.

2. If you are engaging a caterer, be certain he can provide portable refrigeration equipment. If you are arranging the reception yourself, obtain coolers for the wine, other beverages, and food—even inexpensive Styrofoam containers.

3. The menu. Plan on finger food for ease in serving. If food must go unrefrigerated for any length of time, avoid mayonnaise, cream sauces, and custard fillings.

4. The cake. A sugar frosting keeps well, whereas a cream frosting might spoil. Ptomaine-proof your menu.

5. Keep in mind that if you are far from home, there will be no nearby kitchen for your last-minute needs such as a knife or bottle opener. Now is the time to think, plan, check previous chapters and lists so you can pack everything in advance. In addition, will you need any of the following:
> —Folding tables and chairs.
> —Cushions or a plastic tarpaulin.
> —Easy-to-pack plastic wineglasses.

MUSIC

Music helps to create and complete the mood you want—pastoral or solemn or festive. Choose your favorite instruments and selections. Consider the following questions and suggestions:

- —Among the easily portable instruments are guitars, violins, flutes.
- —A small organ can be transported with a little more expense and trouble.
- —If you want your guests to join in the singing or responsive reading, arrange to have copies of their "script" distributed.
- —Do you want background music, dance music, or both?
- —Don't hesitate to accept the offer of talented musical friends if they want to take part in your wedding festivities as instrumentalists or singers. You can send them a thank-you gift and a photo or two of themselves taken at the wedding.

PICTURES

If you neglect having photographs taken on your special day, you will always regret it. A competent friend may be able to cover your wedding. Even if he is donating his services, talk over the not-to-be-missed pictures with him. Provide him with plenty of film, and after the wedding send him a gift as a thank-you for a difficult job well done.

ITEM

Ecology-minded brides have been known to furnish their guests with birdseed in place of traditional rice or rose petals. A combination self-clean product and bird feeder.

Liquid Refreshments Check List

CHECK LIST

These pages will help you organize a cocktail party or a wedding reception. Some hosts prefer to serve champagne or punch and forgo an open bar. Whatever your decision, the reminders are all here.

Quantity Worksheet
- —1 liter serves 22 drinks @ 1½ ounces—7 to 8 persons.
- —1 bottle of wine serves 5 drinks @ 5 ounces. Wineglasses should be only partially filled.
- —1 gallon of wine serves 26 drinks @ 5 ounces.

NOTE: Guests often place their glasses down, forget where, then order a fresh drink. To be safe, figure three drinks per person and an abundance of extra glasses.

Oversupply rather than run short. Nothing need be wasted. At the time you place your order, discuss returns with the store manager. Most bottle shops will credit or exchange the unopened surplus. If you bought at a discount price, however, you might decide to keep the extra for future use.

Set up several bar stations. This will tend to keep people from overcrowding one area.

LIQUID REFRESHMENTS

	NUMBER OF GUESTS	QUANTITY TO ORDER	AMOUNT USED	NUMBER OF GUESTS	QUANTITY TO ORDER	AMOUNT USED
CHAMPAGNE						
SCOTCH						
BOURBON						
VODKA						
GIN						
RUM						
WHITE WINE						
RED WINE						
VERMOUTH						
SHERRY						
DUBONNET						
BEER						
SPRING WATER						
CLUB SODA						
TONIC WATER						
SOFT DRINKS						
FRUIT JUICES						
ICE						
ICE BUCKET						
LEMONS						
LIMES						
OLIVES/ONIONS						
GLASSES						
TOOTH PICKS						
NAPKINS						
COASTERS						
JIGGER						

In addition to one or more bars, waiters can circulate among the guests to take orders.

Instruct bartender. Provide him with a jigger and tell him exactly what strength drinks you wish him to pour.

A Final Thought

All my lists, suggestions, and admonitions are for one purpose—to help you achieve your perfect wedding. Whether you followed tradition or your own ideas, you can feel confident all has been done—everything possible for your start in life together.

Happy Wedding!
Happy Life!

Barbara Lee Follett

Calendar

The wedding date is _____
                          (month)   (date)

This week of _____ is the _____ week
            (month)   (date)

before the wedding.

	Morning	Afternoon	Evening
SUNDAY			
MONDAY			
TUESDAY			
WEDNESDAY			
THURSDAY			
FRIDAY			
SATURDAY			

Calendar

The wedding date is _____
                              (month)   (date)

This week of _____ is the _____ week
                  (month)   (date)

before the wedding.

	Morning	Afternoon	Evening
SUNDAY			
MONDAY			
TUESDAY			
WEDNESDAY			
THURSDAY			
FRIDAY			
SATURDAY			

Calendar

The wedding date is _____
                          (month)   (date)

This week of _____ is the _____ week
              (month)   (date)

before the wedding.

	Morning	Afternoon	Evening
SUNDAY			
MONDAY			
TUESDAY			
WEDNESDAY			
THURSDAY			
FRIDAY			
SATURDAY			

Calendar

The wedding date is _____
                              (month)   (date)

This week of _____ is the _____ week
                  (month)   (date)

before the wedding.

	Morning	Afternoon	Evening
SUNDAY			
MONDAY			
TUESDAY			
WEDNESDAY			
THURSDAY			
FRIDAY			
SATURDAY			

Calendar

The wedding date is _____
                        (month)   (date)

This week of _____ is the _____ week
            (month)   (date)

before the wedding.

	Morning	Afternoon	Evening
SUNDAY			
MONDAY			
TUESDAY			
WEDNESDAY			
THURSDAY			
FRIDAY			
SATURDAY			

Calendar

The wedding date is _____
                        (month)   (date)

This week of _____ is the _____ week
              (month)   (date)

before the wedding.

	Morning	Afternoon	Evening
SUNDAY			
MONDAY			
TUESDAY			
WEDNESDAY			
THURSDAY			
FRIDAY			
SATURDAY			

Calendar

The wedding date is _____
                                     (month)   (date)

This week of _____ is the _____ week
               (month)   (date)

before the wedding.

	Morning	Afternoon	Evening
SUNDAY			
MONDAY			
TUESDAY			
WEDNESDAY			
THURSDAY			
FRIDAY			
SATURDAY			

Calendar

The wedding date is _____
                              (month)   (date)

This week of _____ is the _____ week
                 (month)   (date)

before the wedding.

	Morning	Afternoon	Evening
SUNDAY			
MONDAY			
TUESDAY			
WEDNESDAY			
THURSDAY			
FRIDAY			
SATURDAY			

Notes

Notes

Notes

Notes

Notes

Notes

Notes

Notes

Notes

Notes